BENJAMIN LAY

1677 – 1759

A PIONEER QUAKER ANTISLAVERY
ADVOCATE AND ACTIVIST

HIS 'JOURNAL', LETTERS AND
SUNDRY INFORMATION WITH A
REMEMBRANCE BY ROBERT VAUX

Joshua Evans' Trust 2015

AN INTRODUCTION TO THE JOURNAL, WRITINGS AND ROBERTS VAUX'S *MEMOIR OF THE LIFE OF BENJAMIN LAY*; A PIONEER IN THE EFFORT TO ABOLISH SLAVERY IN NORTH AMERICA

In 1619 nineteen African slaves were brought to Jamestown, Virginia where they were sold in the marketplace. This was the beginning of a practice which proved to be a tragic and traumatic event in the American experience. In the subsequent two hundred forty six years an economic, social, moral and religious struggle centered on the institution of slavery. The rise of the Society of Friends came concurrently with the years when slavery became established on the eastern seaboard. From the earliest of times, the enslavement of indigenous peoples and Africans had become an accepted fact of community life for the majority of European settlers. Numbers of Friends in Quaker meetings were engaged in one form or another in owning slaves or through involvement in the slave trade. Wealth generated by Friends in the slave trade, provides an insight into the truth of the statement "Quakers came to America to do good, and they did well."

A few voices were raised from individual Friends who were to take a stand against slavery. For the most part it took courage to speak out or write against slavery throughout the late seventeenth century to the early eighteenth century. When he made a missionary journey to Barbados in 1671, George Fox witnessed the effects of African slavery at a time when the Island had a large Quaker population. Fox urged that members of the Society treat their slaves humanely and to give them a sound Christian education.

In 1676 the Quaker evangelist William Edmundson came to Barbados proposing that physical slavery and Christian liberty were inconsistent with Truth. He felt that slaves should receive sound religious instruction. His outspoken stand caused hostility from the Quaker planters of Barbados. Later, when he went to Newport, Rhode Island, he learned that Friends there were involved in a lucrative slave trade. To these Friends he expressed the view that slavery "was an oppression of the mind".

Shortly after coming to the Philadelphia region in 1688, German Quakers and Mennonites from Krefeld, Germany sent an antislavery petition to Philadelphia Yearly Meeting. Nothing was to come of this as this petition was 'lost in the shuffle' of Quaker process. In 1698, Robert Pyle, a prosperous Quaker farmer in Chester County had a disturbing dream one night during a time when he felt he should purchase a slave to help around the farm.   He rose in the morning a convinced and passionate abolitionist working to convince others of the evils of slavery.

George Keith was an educated Scots Quaker who moved to Philadelphia. In 1693 he produced the pamphlet *An Exhortation and Caution to Friends concerning Buying or Keeping of Negroes* in which he urged Friends to sign a petition against slavery. The resulting controversy from this effort encouraged Keith to form a splinter group out of Philadelphia Yearly Meeting known as Christian Quakers. He then became so disillusioned that he went back to England, left the Society of Friends and became an Anglican priest.

Two Nantucket Quakers were early advocates for the abolition of slavery. John Farmer spoke so strongly against slavery in the late 1600s that he was disowned by his Meeting. He eventually moved to Philadelphia. In 1715 Elihu Coleman from Nantucket wrote a book entitled *A Testimony Against that Antichristian Practice of Making Slaves of Men*. This was the first antislavery publication to be approved for printing by a monthly meeting.

After remaining silent for thirty years regarding the evils of slavery John Hepburn in 1715 wrote the book *The American Defense of the Christian Golden Rule or an Essay to Prove the Unlawfulness of Making Slaves of Men By Him Who Loves the Freedom of the Souls and Bodies of all Men*. A Quaker from Long Island, William Burling, spoke out against slavery and was disciplined by his meeting for doing so.

Ralph Sandiford came from England, witnessed the brutal slave conditions in Barbados (some of which was meted out by Quaker slave masters). He moved to Philadelphia and became a merchant where his business was located next door to the slave market. He was so distressed by what he witnessed that he moved out into the country, adopted a simple life style which would eschew the use of any products produced by slaves. In 1727 he produced the book:

A Brief Examination of the Practice of the Times, By the Foregoing and the Present Dispensation: Whereby is Manifested, How the Devil Works in the Mystery, Which None Can Understand and Get the Victory Over, But those That Armed with the Light, That Discovers the Temptation and the Author Thereof And Gives Victory Over Him and His Instruments, Who are Now Gone Forth, As in the Beginning, From the True Friends of Jesus, Having the Form of Godliness in Words, But in Deeds Deny the Power Thereof; From Such We Are Commanded to Turn Away.

Ralph Sandiford experienced hostility from the Friends' community through this publication and for his passion in seeking the abolition of slavery. Although ostracized by the Quaker community, he was to have a faithful friend who also had a passion for abolition of all aspects of slavery. This Friend was Benjamin Lay.

Benjamin Lay was a singular individual physically, mentally and socially. He developed a profound passion for the abolition of slavery as a result of his experiences with slavery and the slave trade during the time he was a sailor. In Barbados and then in Philadelphia he developed a profound passion for the abolition of slavery. He used many forms of protest (including 'street theater') to bring the attention of his neighbors and Friends regarding the evils of slavery. Many of his day (even scholars of our day) have described him as being a 'troublemaker' or of 'unsound mind'.

It should be remembered that this small handful of early abolitionists in the Quaker family faced an organization entrenched in and enriched by slavery. Friends had a significant place in American culture in the seventeenth and eighteenth centuries. At one time or another they held economic, social, religious and political power in Barbados (and Charleston, South Carolina where many Barbadians emigrated), New Jersey, North Carolina, Pennsylvania, and Rhode Island. For the most part the Society of Friends were resistant to any change in the social/economic fabric of the times even as it pertained to the issue of slavery.

Benjamin Lay was to bring his disorganized 'journal' and other papers to his friend Benjamin Franklin. Franklin organized and printed the work in a book entitled *All Slave-keepers That Keep the Innocent in Bondage, Apostates.*

Early abolitionists in the Quaker community had a number of things in common. They might be described as radical, catholic, Christian, Quakers: <u>Radical</u> in the meaning of the word *coming from the root or source (e.g.the Sermon on the Mount), basic;* <u>Catholic</u> in the sense of *being universal, all inclusive;* <u>Christian</u> in the *living of Christ's teachings while travelling The Way.* <u>Quaker</u> meaning *one who would live the Truth through the testimony of Friends'.*

During the early period of Quaker settlement the radical witness tended to be evangelical and 'pentecostal' in form. In the later years of the eighteenth century Friends became more settled, 'refined', 'correct' and 'quietistic'. Those who were to support the antislavery movement witnessed in a different manner (often with the approbation of the wider Quaker community). Anthony Benezet, Joshua Evans, John Woolman (and other Friends) tempered their passion through a more gentle approach; being firm yet taking special care to honor the slave as well as the slave-holder as children of God. Common among these witnesses for universal justice was a deep appreciation for the practice of good stewardship and active reconciliation. There was a deep concern for creatures and creation, for ordering life to be sensitive regarding the use of the things that might have roots in exploitation and oppression.

Those in this ministry were prone to visions and dreams. Woolman would write of this in his *Journal*. Joshua Evans detailed one particular dream (or nightmare) that depicted a world turned upside down and torn apart as a result of slavery. (This was to be excised by Friends' editors from being included in the printing of his *Journal*.) Common among these witnesses was the feeling that if the institution of slavery were to continue the result would be horrendous violence in future times.

Note: When our worship study group considered what might be included in *A Book of Discipline*. It was felt that we should acknowledge the fact that slavery exists in a greater degree in our time than ever before. We included a statement regarding this in the text with a footnote that: "Friends were early pioneers in the efforts to abolish slavery. We are reminded that slavery still exists in the world today to a greater degree than in earlier times. Slavery comes in many forms: chattel slavery, human trafficking, wage and debt slavery, conscription, sexual slavery, child slavery, illiteracy, addiction slavery, etc. We are urged to renew our deep concern and work for the abolition of all forms of slavery in our time." The concern is that we not be comfortably complacent regarding this important testimony in the present and future as had been true in the past.

It was felt that by developing a module around the issue of slavery for *A School for Living: ...* (under the aegis of *Joshua Evans' Trust*) we might consider how we might understand and become involved as modern day abolitionists in working to end all forms of slavery.   This module could be one way of honoring Benjamin Lay through an institute honoring him in speaking to this concern.   The module could be medium of educating ourselves about ancient and modern slavery, of action needed (including 'street theatre') and other means in speaking 'Truth to Power' regarding all forms of slavery in the human experience.

We adopted and updated the wording of that wonderful hymn written by 'The Quaker Poet', John Greenleaf Whittier, who was an ardent abolitionist of the nineteenth century. The hymn can be sung to the tune *O Perfect Love* or *Vesalius*:

> Neighbor and friend, fold to thy heart another;
> Where kindness dwells, the peace of God is there;
> To worship rightly is to love each other,
> Each smile a hymn, each kindly deed a prayer.

> For them whom Jesus loved has truly spoken;
> The holier worship which God seeks to bless
> Restores the lost, and binds the spirit broken,
> And feeds the widow and the fatherless.

> Follow with reverent steps the great example,
> Of him whose holy work was doing good;
> So shall the wide earth be God's holy temple,
> Each loving life a psalm of gratitude.

> Then shall all shackles fall, the stormy clangor---
> Of wild war carnage o'er the earth shall cease.
> Love shall tread out the baleful fire of anger,
> And in its ashes plant the tree of peace.

(The following material from the writings of Benjamin Lay has been condensed, the spelling updated--yet maintaining British colonial spellings of some words, and by changing some words into expressions more understandable to the modern reader.)

(One of the best historical studies regarding slavery is David Brion Davis' book *The Problem of Slavery in Western Culture* which won the Pulitzer Prize in 1967.)

MEMOIR OF THE LIFE OF BENJAMIN LAY AN EARLY PUBLIC ADVOCATE FOR THE EMANCIPATION OF THE ENSLAVED AFRICANS

ROBERTS VAUX

Philadelphia – Published in 1858

PREFACE

The design of this Introduction is not to make the customary apologies of authorship, nor to furnish in justification of this publication, a variety of ingenious reasons, which may have had no influence with the writer.

*His sole object, and the utmost extent of his views has been, to furnish whatever his feeble efforts could contribute toward rescuing from unmerited forgetfulness, the name and services of **Benjamin Lay** who, in his opinion, deserve to be held in honourable estimation, so long as it is admitted that* memory is performing her noblest office when aiding the obligations of gratitude and justice.

The subsequent memoirs will not introduce the reader to the knowledge of men and women who have distinguished themselves as struggling in the battle which is "with confused noise, and garments rolled in blood,"---who have attained a rank among the luminaries of science, or have been elevated to notice by a splendid career of senatorial greatness; features in the human character which generally excite the respect of nations, awaken the admiration, and beget the applause of humankind---and secure to such as appear in those higher spheres of action, the certainty of biographical honour. But with those who, with the author, believe in the truth that the individuals whose services it is his purpose now to delineate and record, have the fairest claims to the respect of the human race.

Among the events which occasionally appear in the history of nations, to dignify and adorn their character, and shed over them a ray of genuine greatness and glory, the abolition of the African slave trade must be admitted to hold a conspicuous place. It was one of the purest offerings ever borne by lawgivers to the altar of justice---the most acceptable tribute which legislative power could pay at the shrine of mercy. Whilst, however, it is customary to admire the wisdom, and applaud the virtue of those governments which have wiped such pollution from their name, it should equally be a pleasure and a duty, to recognize the labours of individuals in that noble cause of reformation and *benevolence. It would be difficult to calculate precisely how extensive and availing the efforts of a man might be, in correcting the opinions of a large community, especially if their exertions should be so much in opposition to the interests, the habits, and sentiments of a people, as to excite towards them the spirit of intolerance and persecution. This remark is certainly applicable to the history of Benjamin Lay, who is among the first of the very few in any country that had just conceptions of the rights of the enslaved Africans, and sufficient firmness to avow their opinions concerning the cruelty which was triumphantly exercised over that oppressed race.*

At the period when he went forth distributing their essays, proclaiming the iniquity inseparable from the trade in human flesh, and showing the inconsistency which marked the conduct of Christians, who held their fellow creatures in bondage, the opposition to their views and wishes was so general and so intense, that it is believed from that cause the intellect of those remarkable men became partially affected. But who will question that they were instrumental (at a great sacrifice indeed) in laying the foundation of the change of opinion, which afterward became universal in this commonwealth, and spread its benign influence through neighbouring states, and to remote nations.

Of those, therefore, for whom they did so much, in order to persuade them to be just to themselves, and to their afflicted to other human beings, it is fair to enquire---have you repaid the measure of justice due to your benefactors?--- Candour must reply in the negative. No memorial invites the eye to that which mingles with their mortal relics---no volume records the story of his eccentric and devoted life. The place of their residence---their nature of their occupations---the habitations where their earthly pilgrimage was closed, have been involved in doubt and uncertainly---and now indistinctly linger upon the recollection of most of the few remaining individuals, who were in the morning of life, when old age and disease terminated their existence. In searching for information respecting Benjamin Lay, visits were made to most of the oldest inhabitants in the neighbourhoods where they had lived. The combined ages of ten of those persons amounts to eight hundred and twenty-one years, and it is remarkable, that all these ancient people appeared to enjoy unusual health and strength, and in most instances then faculties were unimpaired. On enquiring, several of them said, they had observed through life great temperance in drinking.

Notwithstanding the disadvantages which attended the collection of materials for his biography, at this remote period from the time in which he lived, and the consequent paucity of matter which could be procured for the purpose; these causes have not operated to discourage the publication of the fragments which were gathered.

The result, which as it is, is now submitted to the public, as a sincere tribute to the memory of Benjamin Lay, ---an effort, the best which it was in the power of the author to make, to perpetuate the recollection of his virtues.

MEMOIRS OF BENJAMIN LAY: Benjamin Lay was born at Colchester, in the County of Essex, Great Britain, Anno Domini 1677. His parents, who were members of the Society of Friends, carefully instructed him in the religious principles which they professed, but their poor resources did not enable them to bestow upon their son, more than the rudiments of learning, as taught in the lower order of English schools. At an early period of his youth, he was placed an apprentice with a glove-maker, in whose service he continued for some time. Before he had attained his nineteenth year, he abandoned this employment and went to reside on a farm in the tenure of his brother. In this situation he remained until the independence which the age of manhood confers, permitted him to gratify the leading inclination of his mind, which withdrew him from the interesting and innocent employments of agriculture, to encounter the hardships and perils of the life of a sailor.

Whilst thus employed he visited various sections of the globe. In a memorandum he relates, that he served eighteen months on board a ship of four hundred tons burden, in a voyage to Scanderoon (Alexandria in Syria, now known as Iskenderun), and it is probable that during the stay of the vessel at that port, he made an excursion to the interior of Syria; for he often related, among other incidents connected with his ocean wandering, that he had visited the memorable spot, where Jesus conversed with the woman of

Samaria, and had refreshed himself by a drink of water from Jacob's well. His maritime employment terminated in 1710, when he was married to one of his countrywomen, and settled in the town of his nativity. But little is known concerning him during several years of this part of his life, excepting that he appears to have taken an interest in some of the public topics and controversies, by which the close of the seventeenth and commencement of the eighteenth centuries were distinguished. He presented, in person to George the First, and George the Second a copy of John Milton's pamphlet entitled *Considerations touching the likeliest means to remove hirelings out of the Church* and on the occasion of the last of these interviews, he was admitted to a private audience of the royal family. To what extent, and in what manner, he participated in the contests of the times, cannot now be accurately ascertained. It is fair to presume, however, that he exceeded the bounds which limited his brothers and sisters in religious community; for in the year 1717 they were induced to disunite him from membership among them, and as no charge of immoral conduct was ever made against him, this measure is probably to be attributed to the part which he took in the controversies just mentioned.

As he approaches nearer to us by the lapse of time, traits of his character are developed, which establish the belief that he was one of those extraordinary men, whose career through life excited observation an alarm. If the comparison be admissible, he appeared rather like the comet, which threatens, in its irregular course, the destruction of the worlds near which it passes, then as one of those tranquil orbs which hold their accustomed place, and dispense their light, in the harmonious order of heaven.

In 1718, at the age of forty-one years, he removed from his native land to the island of Barbados, and there established himself in mercantile business. Here he is exhibited in a new and interesting field of action, in which he appears to have taken a bold and decided part. At this period, the African slave trade was carried on, if possible, with more intense cruelty, than at any previous or subsequent stage of its uniformly iniquitous history. The treatment to which the unhappy victims of avarice were subjected in the service of their masters, on the plantations of the West Indian Islands, furnished a melancholy proof of the application of human ingenuity exerted in the contrivance of the most barbarous punishments, ---as well as the absence of all compassion, from the hearts of those whose mandate directed, and whose power inflicted them. Thus a witness of scenes which were calculated to excite the keenest sensibility, and awaken the tenderest sympathy of his nature, Benjamin Lay became singularly enlightened, in relation to the injustice and oppression exercised toward the people of Africa. From that moment, every faculty of his mind was exerted, to render odious, not only in the opinion of the community in which he lived, but among mankind universally, a traffic which begot so much crime---entailed so much misery---and threatened such awful retribution from the Omnipotent and Parent of the whole human family.

We now find this philanthropic advocate of the oppressed, fearlessly engaged in public and private admonition with all who were in any degree implicated in the crime of enslaving their species; and whilst he zealously pleaded with the oppressor for the extension of clemency, he was equally conspicuous for the practical benevolence which he manifested toward the subjects of his compassion. Whenever he met the slaves of the island, he noticed them with kindness and commiseration. They soon became generally acquainted with his views and exertions in their favour, and as an evidence of gratitude to their benefactor, they came from the neighbouring farms on the Sabbath day and assembled around his house in the town, to the number of many hundreds; and he thus had an opportunity of conveying to them suitable advice, and also of furnishing them gratuitously with simple and wholesome food, as liberally as his restricted resources would allow. In this practice he continued, until popular clamour was raised against him, and he was denied even the melancholy satisfaction of showing his tenderness for those, whose sufferings, at most, he could only mitigate. In proportion to the steadiness and determination of his testimony against African bondage, was the hostility of those who were enriched by its existence. Their opposition to his truly Christian principles at length became o violent, that after having endured the conflict for several years, and perceiving no prospect of effecting any change in the conduct of the slave-holders, he resolved to seek an asylum in another country. This resolution, when communicated to his wife, she entirely approved.

Her mind was deeply affected with the subject of slavery, and she said on that occasion, "that she wished to leave Barbados, lest by remaining there she might be leavened into the nature of the inhabitants, which was pride and oppression." After having resided thirteen years in Barbados, he came to Philadelphia in 1731.

Having followed him to the shores of our own country, it may be proper, before proceeding farther in his history, to furnish a description of his personal appearance; for his physical organization was not less remarkable than the qualities of his mind were rare and extraordinary. He was only four feet seven inches in height; his head was large in proportion to his body; the features of his face were remarkable, and boldly delineated, and his countenance was grave and benign. He was hunch-backed, with a projecting chest, below which his body became much contracted. His legs were so slender, as to appear almost unequal to the purpose of supporting him, diminutive as his frame was, in comparison with the ordinary size of human stature. A habit he had contracted, of standing in a twisted position, with one hand resting upon his left hip, added to the effect produced by a large white beard, that for many years had not been shaved, contributed to render his figure perfectly unique. It is singular, that his wife very much resembled him in size, having a crooked back like her husband, and the similarity of their appearance even excited the remarks of the slaves in Barbados, who used to say when they saw them together, *"That little backararar* (name for Europeans or white people) *man, go all over world, see for that bacararar woman for himself."*

On his arrival in Pennsylvania, it was soon discovered that his character was eccentric. The practice of holding slaves was general in the province, though they were treated more mildly than their debased countrymen in the West Indies. Lay was, however, established in the pious doctrine that the odious system of slavery was altogether unrighteous, and with the same zeal with which he had begun, he continued to reprobate the conduct of everyone who participated in the custom. His independence of opinion, and freedom of expression, rendered him a less welcome emigrant than those who could quietly approve, or openly adopt the habits of the times, and his sentiments met with vigorous opposition from every quarter. This this champion of justice, of human rights, and reformation, found himself again an almost solitary combatant in a field where prejudice and avarice, had marshalled their combined forces against him. His disappointment at being thus received in Philadelphia, the very name of which promised tranquility and repose to his long afflicted heart, gave a new, and as was at first supposed, a misanthropic determination to his mind. His intention, when he left Barbados, was to have resided in the city, but he now resolved to fix his residence in a more retired place in the country.

In conformation with this plan, he procured a few acres of land, situate between Germantown and the old York road, about six miles north of Philadelphia, and not far distant from the present village of

Mileston. On the rural spot of his choice, he built a cottage, resembling, in its construction, a cave, planted a small orchard, and for utility and ornament, cultivated near the front of his humble dwelling several walnut trees, which remain venerable and living monuments of the place of his first habitation in Pennsylvania.

Having completed his house, he removed to it in 1732. He now adopted habits of the most rigid temperance, self-denial, and frugality, which he ever after observed. He drank nothing but water and milk, and subsisted altogether upon vegetable diet. His clothing was entirely composed of tow fabric, of his own spinning, and of natural colour. His tender conscience would not permit him to eat any food, nor wear any garment, nor use any article which was procured at the expense of animal life, or that was in the remotest degree, the product of the labour of slaves. This purified, by what he conceived to be obligatory and necessary to qualify him for the great duty assigned him, he went forth with fresh animation to disseminate his principles. Excepting the time requisite for procuring food and raiment, he was altogether devoted to the ministry of his doctrines; and for the promotion of them he visited several of the governors of the neighbouring provinces, as well as other influential characters, in church and state. He omitted no opportunity to endeavor to interest everyone with whom he met in the benevolent work he had undertaken; and to effect this, he adopted various means---some of which were so extravagant as to induce the belief that his intellect was partially diseased. Although he had been dis united from membership with the Society of Friends at an early period of his life, yet he always avowed their principles, and was attached to them as a religious community; but he could not endure the idea, that professing as they did, it was proper that any of them should hold their fellow beings in bondage; hence, he appears to have directed the most energetic and unceasing assaults upon them; nor could he be persuaded that it must, from the very nature and constitution of the human mind, be a gradual work, if ever they were cleansed as a people from the practice, which, even at that time, some of them with himself, considered as an offence in the sight of Divine Purity.

The following facts will show some of the modes he adopted, to convince the Society of Friends, and others, of the impropriety of their conduct in keeping slaves. During the session of an annual meeting, held at Burlington in New Jersey, Benjamin Lay proceeded to that city. Having previously prepared a sufficient quantity of the juice of pokeberry (*Phytolacca decandrea*) to fill a bladder, he contrived to conceal it within the cover of a large folio volume, the leaves of which were removed. He then put on a military coat, and belted a small sword by his side; over the whole of this dress he threw his great coat, which was made in the most simple manner, and secured it upon himself with; a single button. Thus equipped, he entered the meetinghouse and placed himself in a conspicuous situation, from which he addressed the audience in substance as follows:

> "Oh all you slave masters who are contentedly holding your fellow creatures in a state of slavery

during life, well knowing the cruel sufferings those innocent captives undergo in their state of bondage, both in these North American colonies, and in the West India islands; you must know they are not made slaves by any direct law, but are held by an arbitrary and self-interested custom, in which you participate. And especially you profess '*to do unto others as ye would they should do unto you*'---and yet, in direct opposition to every principle of reason, humanity, and religion, you are forcibly retaining your fellow humanity, from one generation to another, in a state of unconditional servitude; you might as well throw off the plain coat as I do"---(here he loosed the button, and the great coat falling behind him, his warlike appearance was exhibited to his astonished audience) and proceeded---"It would be as justifiable in the sight of the Almighty, who beholds and respects all nations and colours of men and women with equal regard, if you should thrust a sword through their hearts as I do through this book." He then drew his sword and pierced the bladder, sprinkling its contents over those who sat near him.

On another occasion, when a deep snow was on the ground, he stationed himself at the gateway, opening to one of their meetinghouses, having his right leg and foot entirely uncovered;; as the people went in, several of them reasoned with him for thus exposing himself, and cautioned him against the danger of contracting disease by such conduct. "Ah (said Lay,) you pretend compassion for me, but you do not feel for the poor slaves in your fields, who go all winter half clad." For the purpose of enforcing upon the mind of a neighbor of his, with whom he had often remonstrated, a conviction of his guiltiness in keeping a slave, Benjamin adopted a plan which evinced his knowledge of human nature. This man had an interesting child, a boy of six years old, whom

Lay sometimes met at a distance from the dwelling of his parents; on one of those occasions he succeeded in decoying him to his cave, about one mile distant, within which, by means of some amusement, contrived to keep the boy concealed from view. As the evening came on, Lay observed the father and mother running towards his dwelling; as they drew near, discovering their distress, he advanced and met them, enquiring in a feeling manner. "What is the matter?"---the afflicted parents, apprehensive that they should never recover their child, replied with anguish: "Oh Benjamin, Benjamin! Our child is gone, he has been missing all day." Benjamin Lay paused, and said, "Your child is safe in my house, and you may now conceive of the sorrow you inflict upon the parents of the slave gal you hold in slavery, for she was torn from them by avarice."

In the year 1737, he published a book entitled *All Slave Keepers that Keep the Innocent in bondage, Apostates.* This work contains many interesting facts, and some powerful appeals to the judgment and feelings. In some parts, however, it manifests the same intolerance of the mistakes of others, which characterizes the other productions of the author on the subject of slavery, and which, at the time of this publication, was calculated, by the obstinacy, which it was likely to excite, rather to confirm than remove the error of some of those whom it was addressed. He distributed his book gratuitously, particularly among those who were about to succeed the generation which was then passing away; and there can be no doubt that his conscientious efforts made a deep and useful impression upon most persons who read what he had written, with the attention which it certainly merited. On the last page of this book, Benjamin Lay gives a critic on his own labours; and the candour, simplicity, and humility with which it is clothed, furnish conclusive evidence of the sincerity and urbanity of this character.

Not long before he removed from his cave, curiosity, associated with respect for him, induced Governor Richard Penn, Dr. Benjamin Franklin and some other gentlemen to make a visit to Lay---he received them in his primitive home with his usual politeness; after some interesting conversation, the table was spread for dinner, and plentifully covered with vegetables and fruit, of which he thus invited them to partake saying, "This is not the kind of fare you have at home, but it is good enough for you or me---and such as it is, you are welcome to eat of it."

Having passed the sixty-third year of his age, he began to feel some of the infirmities incident to the decline of life, which, connected with the incessant application of his time to his favourite subject, and the desire to memorialize his wife Sarah Lay to whom he was most tenderly attached might be relieved from the domestic cares which she had been long engaged with, influenced him to leave the large home they had lived in for more than nine miles. (Sarah Lay was an intelligent and pious woman and an approved minister of the gospel in the Society of Friends who suffered by witnessing for the injustice of the custom of human bondage.) They moved a few miles to the farm of John Phipps in whose family they boarded, near Abington meetinghouse. Soon after this change of residence, the interesting and endeared connection which had subsisted between this affectional pair, was dissolved by the death of Sarah. This event, which involved him in great affliction, was rendered more acute by the circumstance that he had no children, or other relative, to participate in his sorrow---to share his loss---to yield the sympathy which such a loss demanded---or afford the consolation and aid that a bereavement so severe required.

The loss he had suffered, and his advanced age might be supposed sufficient to have abated the ardour of his mind, and prevented him from active exertion. But Benjamin Lay was no ordinary man. He rose to the influence of such causes and actively resumed his labours of benevolence. He continued to publish and circulate essays on the subject of slavery, and sought for occasions, both publicly and privately, to speak of its injustice. For this purpose he attended all places of public worship, without regard to the religious professions of their congregations. On one occasion, he walked into the Oxford church, with a mantle of sack cloth wrapped round him, and stood attentively listening to the sermon. When the services of the morning were over, Lay thus began an address to the congregation: "I do not approve of all the minister has said, but I did not come here to find fault with the preaching; I came to cry aloud against your practice of slave holding." In all the places of worship which he thus visited, he used the same freedom; and his addresses were sometimes so long and vehement as to require his removal from the meetinghouse; an act to which he always submitted without opposition.

Persons, who were not acquainted with him, often deceived themselves by supposing him to be destitute of common understanding. In company he would often make observations and remarks, calculated to provoke argument, with a view to fathom the minds of those with whom he conversed; and the estimate of their characters was formed with astonishing facility and correctness. His replies were always pointed, and strictly adapted to the nature of the questions proposed; for he instantly discovered whether an inquiry was made with a desire to obtain information, or suggested to gratify mere curiosity, and produce ridicule. He was also scrupulously careful to respect the truth, in all his conversation, and would rebuke those who in the least degree departed from it by the use of words and phrases, complimentary or otherwise, which did not proceed from the heart. As he was once walking from his home to Philadelphia, he was met by several persons on horseback, who unwisely expected he would afford them diversion. One of the party stopped him with this salutation---"Sir, your humble servant"---Lay looked upon the stranger, and said, "If thou art my humble servant, clean my shoes." Not sufficiently ascertained of his character by that remark, they tauntingly inquired of him which was the direct route to heaven. Lay promptly replied---"Do justly, love mercy, and walk humbly with your God." They were then satisfied without further interrogation, and left him, evidently mortified at their impotent efforts to produce idle merriment, by insult upon real virtue.

He always travelled on foot, and made frequent visits in the nighbourhood, as well as at a considerable distance from home; having once walked to Philadelphia, with an intention of conversing with an individual of considerable note, he found the family, on his arrival, sitting at breakfast; Lay entered the room, and was invited to partake with them, but seeing a black servant in attendance, he inquired of his master, "Is this man a slave?" Being answered affirmatively, he said, "then I will not share with thee the fruits of thy unrighteousness," and immediately departed from the house. He never owned a slave himself, neither would he sit with, nor partake of the food of anyone who kept them. Notwithstanding the populate antipathy against Lay, he enjoyed the friendship and society of some of the most pious and learned men, who at that time adorned the province of Pennsylvania. The most cordial attachment subsisted between him and the truly honourable Anthony Benezet a foremost leader in the antislavery movement. He maintained through life, an uninterrupted interchange with Dr. Benjamin Franklin, the Universalist preacher Dr. George DeBenneville, and many other distinguished characters. He was also intimately acquainted with Ralph Sandiford, who, like himself was an ardent oppose of slavery and wrote upon the subject.

Benjamin Lay's mind was not exclusively directed to the subject of the trade in human flesh and the shocking train of evils by which it was attended; it observed, and investigated other objects connected with the interests of civil society and the welfare of humankind.   His attention was directed to a consideration of the nature and humane treatment of prisoners for offenses against the laws.   The ideas which, within thirty years led to the melioration of the penal code of Pennsylvania. These thoughts were expressed by Lay, as long since as the year 1737, ---at that time he thus notices the subject: "as to criminals, they had better be kept in bondage, that by labour they might be brought to repentance and amendment of life, in order to a happy death, rather than to put them to death in their offenses; for in the grave there is no repentance. Hard labour and simple living is an antidote to luxury and idleness, and captivity the reverse of nature, might prevent a great deal of wickedness in the world. This I should rejoice to see." This judicious, enlightened, and truly Christian sentiment, is of itself an imperishable evidence of the profound conceptions of his understanding, and alone sufficient, if there were no other proof of his desire to promote the happiness of his fellow humans, to entitle them to respect and gratitude of the whole of mankind.

With the same enlightened zeal, he pointed out the pernicious consequences which would result from the introduction of foreign spirits into this country. He declared that the general use of them would corrupt and degrade any people, and that there was danger, if they could be easily and cheaply procured, of their becoming the habitual beverage of the inhabitants. He introduces the subject, in considering the trade which at that day was extensively carried on with the West Indies; and says, "We send away our excellent provisions and other good things, to purchase such filthy stuff, which tends to the corruption of humankind, and they send us some of their incorrigible slaves, which the slave traders cannot rule themselves, along with their rum to complete the tragedy; that is to say, to destroy the people in Pennsylvania, and ruin the country."

In fulfilling the purposes of his universal ministry, he devoted a portion of his time to visiting schools, and embraced every proper opportunity of impressing the susceptible minds of children with a just and reverent sense of their duties toward God--- enforcing the importance of early establishing themselves in habits of order, sobriety, and frugality---inculcating the principles of humanity by simple illustrations, and recommending it to them to be governed through life by these precepts, and to follow the meek and humble example of our holy Redeemer. The following feeling observation is from the pen of an ancient and worthy gentleman, who in his early youth was a member of one of the schools that Lay frequented; "When the children were reading in the Bible, he would stop them and explain particular passages for their improvement, and although we at that time thought too lightly of Benjamin's anxiety for our welfare, yet some of his labours and admonitions are remembered (by one at least of the scholars,) at the present day, though his advice was imparted more than sixty years ago."

Benjamin Lay had no compassion for vagrant mendicants; he used frequently to assert that "anyone who is able to go abroad and beg, can earn four-pence a day, and that is, enough to keep a person above want or dependence in this country." He was nevertheless charitable toward those who by disease, or misfortune, were reduced to necessitous circumstances, and among the numerous instances of his judicious dispensation of money, the following is worthy of notice. He understood that a poor woman in the neighbourhood, was in need of relief, and to ascertain the fact, called upon a respectable person whom he supposed to be acquainted with the particulars of her situation. Having thus satisfied himself of the truth of the case, he presented to the person on whom he had called several silver pieces--- saying, "lay this out for her, but don't let it be known where it came from."

His fondness for frequent retirement and meditation, continued throughout his life; and for the more complete indulgence and enjoyment of this rational habit, he selected an interesting spot, on the farm of the person with whom he resided, and improved a natural excavation in the earth, near a fine spring of water, so as to afford himself a commodious home. The interior part of the roof of is 'cave' was neatly ornamented with festoons of evergreen, and in the other respects, the room was conveniently fitted for his purpose. Here was kept his library of books, which amounted to near two hundred volumes, comprising some of the works of the best authors in theology, biography, poetry, and history. In that seclusion he reflected, read, and wrote.

After Lay's death the principal part of his manuscripts were preserved by the gentleman with whom he lived, but it is sincerely to be lamented that those relics fell into the hands of the British, during the revolutionary war, who, it is supposed, destroyed them. His books were disposed of at the sale of his effects. Two of these volumes have, after considerable search, been lately discovered. They contain numerous marginal annotations, from which, for want of better sources whence to derive a knowledge of the reflections of this Christian philosopher, a few of his most interesting remarks are known.

His precepts were generally sound, and uniformly supported by the weighty sanction of practice. Whatever he conceived to be his duty. That he performed at every hazard. He persuaded, admonished, and threatened without fear or flattery.

One of the most extraordinary acts of his life, was the attempt he made, in imitation of the Saviour of humankind, to fast for the term of forty days. Perhaps no Christian professor, except himself, ever conceived the fast of our Saviour to be intended as an example for humankind. We must not, however, rashly condemn the conduct of Lay. He certainly acted from a sense of duty; and the voluntary penance to which he subjected himself, is at least a proof of resolute self-denial, and of the power of the human system to sustain itself under a deprivation of its accustomed subsistence. He persisted in his fast for three weeks. For several days after he had commenced it, he continued to pursue his common occupations. He rose at his usual time, which was always at the dawn of day, took his usual exercise, and made his usual excursions in the neighbourhood. One morning he even walked to Philadelphia, where he had an interview with Dr. Franklin, who has often been heard to remark that on that occasion Lay's breath was so acrid as to produce a suffusion of water in his eyes, which was extremely painful. The following memorandum will show what Benjamin Lay's feelings were at the time it was made: "25th of 12th. Mo. 1737-8, this being the ninth day of my fasting, having taken nothing but spring water several times a day, and am as well in health, as ever, since I came to Pennsylvania." Soon after this his strength began to fail. He was at length unable to leave his chamber, and finally, was confined to his bed. When he could no longer help himself, he directed a large loaf of bread to be placed on a table near to him, and upon this he kept his eyes steadily fixed. He conversed very little, but he often addressed himself in these words: "Benjamin thou seest it, but thou shalt not eat it."

Vain were the concerns of his friends to induce him to abandon his fast; his mind was immoveable, notwithstanding all their representations, that if he persisted much longer, he would certainly perish. With the rapid sinking of his system, his mental faculties began to fail. As soon as this was perceived by those around him, they administered suitable diet, and thus he was gradually restored.

During the last one or two years of the close of his life, the infirmities of age disqualified him for much exertion, either of body or mind. He remained principally at home, employed in spinning and other domestic occupations. Honey was one of the few articles of his food, and he amused himself with constructing hives for the accommodation of his bees, and observing their curious labour. By his friendly care to those industrious insects, and by abstaining from the cruel practice of destroying them in order to procure their honey, he increased his original family to a large community whose dwellings extended more than a hundred feet in a continued line*.

To a person who went to see him in the last year of his life, he offered to secure one hundred pounds, if he would engage, after his death, to burn his body, and throw the ashes into the sea. He assigned no reason for the wish which dictated this singular proposition, and the individual to whom the application was made declining the office, he never after mentioned it.

Not long before his death, a friend of Lay's made him a visit for the purpose of acquainting him that the Religious Society of Friends had come to the determination to disown such of their members as could not be persuaded to desist from

--*It is noteworthy that Benjamin Lay's hive construction followed the African way of keeping bees as the bees were not destroyed in harvesting the honey (which suggests that he knew of African agricultural traditions). The European and colonial practice was to destroy the bee skep and the bees in harvesting the honey.

the practice of holding slaves, or were concerned in the importation of them. The venerable and constant friend and advocate of that oppressed people, attentively listened to this heart-cheering message, and after a few moments of reflection on what he had heard, he rose from his chair, and in an attitude of devotional reverence, poured forth this prayer: "Thanksgiving and praise be rendered unto the Lord God." After a short pause, he added---"I can now die in peace."

Thus were his feelings sublimed by the solemn conviction of the controlling influence of God. To him he considered the acknowledgment due, for this change in the conduct of Friends, and to him was it fervently offered. At this interesting period, Lay's mind also appears to have conceived the prophetic and joyful anticipation, that as he had lived to witness an event which he so ardently desired, and so faithfully labored to promote, he would now be permitted to close in tranquility his career on earth. This expectation was soon realized; for a short time after, being absent from home, he was suddenly taken ill. In consequence of this event, several of his neighbours met for the purpose of devising what could best be done for him in his actual situation. Among these was his friend Joshua Morris, whom Lay observing, several times requested that he might be taken to his home. He was at length conveyed thither. The continued violence of his disease convinced those around him that it would terminate his life, and Lay himself was fully sensible of his impending death. He therefore directed his attention to some necessary arrangements with regard to his worldly affairs, and by a verbal will, gave to the Society of Friends at Abington, the sum of forty pounds, to be appropriated to the education of the poor children of that meeting. About two weeks after his attack, he peacefully surrendered his life to Him who gave it, on the 3d. of the 2d. month 1759 at the age of 82. During 41 years, 28 of which were passed in Pennsylvania he had continued his zealous testimony against African slavery.

His remains were interred in Friend's burial ground at Abington; and the inventory of his effects, taken after his decease, indicated his estate to be worth five hundred and eighteen pounds, twelve shillings and nine pence, all of which was personal property.

A respectful consideration for the opinions of those whose eye may trace the story of his life, as here delineated would teach the propriety of leaving this duty to be performed by the unbiased exercise of every reader's judgment. This right the author of this biography would be happy to make a favourable impression concerning the life of Benjamin Lay.

He was certainly a man eminently endowed with strong natural abilities; but his intellectual powers were not expanded by an education founded upon the basis of liberal learning, nor was his mind polished and refined by the embellishments of ornamental literature. His knowledge of humankind was extensive, but to the polite accomplishments of the world, he paid little regard. It is not therefore surprising, that in the support of hi strong opinions, he was obstinate. He had a strong temperament, but it was always excited for mercy's sake, and in behalf of those who dared or could not assert their own rights. His eccentricity was remarkable, but, in the main, it served the purposes of utility. His habits, though singular, were in many respects worthy of imitation. All must acknowledge that "oppression will make the wise man mad." He was pious and benevolent as most would admit. That he was generous, few can deny. That his opinions were correct, concerning the great work of reformation and in speaking for the slaves of which he was one of the founders, we have the almost universal consent of humankind, in the honourable verdict which civilized nations have pronounced upon the question.

ALL SLAVE-KEEPERS That keep the Innocent in Bondage, APOSTATES Pretending to lay Claim to the Pure and Holy Christian Religion; of what Congregation soever, but especially in their Ministers, by whose example the filthy Leprosy and Apostacy is spread far and near, it is a notorious Sin, which many of the true Friends of Christ, and his pure Truth, called *Quakers,* has been for many Years, and still are concerned to write and bear Testimony against; as a Practice so gross and hurtful to Religion, and destructive to Government, beyond what Words can set forth, or can be declared of by Men or Angels, and yet lived in by Ministers and Magistrates in *America.*

The Leaders of the People cause them to Err.

Written for a General Service, by him that truly and sincerely desires the present and eternal Welfare and Happiness of all Mankind, all the World over, of all Colours, and Nations, as his own Soul;

Benjamin Lay, Philadelphia;

(Printed for the Author. 1737)

THE PREFACE

Impartial Reader: *These Things following are so far from offending or grieving my very dear true and tender Friends, called Quakers, who love the Truth more than all, that it is by their request and desire that they are made public; for I can say in the Truth before the Lord, that I love them in and for the Truth's sake, and covet their sweet Unity, and pure Fellowship in the Gospel, their sweet Unity, and pure Fellowship in the Gospel, more than my natural Life, and all things in the World, without it or them, my record is in Heaven.*

I say for the Truth, and Friends sake, these things are exposed, and I myself likewise, although not without some fear and trembling, for fear I should hurt Truth's cause, which is God's cause, I being and seeing myself so very unfit almost every way, as a Man, yet I can truly say as a Christian, I believed it my Duty, but made not haste, for the Lord my good God, the Truth knows, that I have prayed unto him earnestly, many Days and Nights, with great concern of mind, that he would be pleased to raise up and concern some worthy Friend or other, of more repute and Esteem amongst Men; for I know myself to be so very mean and contemptible in the sight of Men, almost in every respect, so that I might and do much question the Event, but shall leave that to the Lord, to whom faithfulness and obedience is required; and no true Peace without it. For I have found long ago, the saying of Truth verified, He that loves anything mor than me, is not worthy of me: I have often thought of Moses' Prayer, and Gideon's request, when the Lord was about to send them to deliver his People from Captivity, and many other worthy Men, ay, and Women to, which are mentioned in Holy writ, and many Thousands more no doubt, which we have no Account of there, for it is believed, we have but a very small part of what have been written, and yet full enough, if we will but be faithful; my dear tender and well beloved Friends, I beg, I pray, and beseech us, let us be more faithful I entreat, in bowels of Love, let us be faithful, let us be faithful, let us be faithful to God in all things; and then I know blessed be his pure Name, which is the Truth, that when the Scourge shall come, he will secure us in Life or in Death; and that will be enough for us, so be it, saith my Soul, and is in humble request. **Benjamin Lay**

Abington, Philadelphia County, in Pennsylvania, the 17th, 9th Month, 1736

ALL SLAVE-KEEPERS, ETC: In 1718 William Burling, now living, for aught I know, on Long Island, made some Observations concerning Slave-keeping. This was the same Year I was convinced of the same Hellish Practice, I then living in Barbados. *Benjamin Lay.*

An Address to the Elders of the Church, upon the occasion of some Friends compelling certain Persons, and their posterity, to serve them continually and arbitrarily, without Regard to Equity or Right, not heeding whether they give them anything near so much as their Labour deserveth.

My Dear Beloved Friends, and Elder Brethren and Sisters, whom as it behoves me, I would entreat as Fathers, a weighty Concern from the Lord, is and hath been at times for many Years on my Spirit, in consideration of this unchristian Liberty, being indulged in the Church, for it is in itself none of the least of the World's Corruptions, [no, say I, but the greatest Evil bought into the Church in America;] and indeed God manifested the Evil to me before I was 12 Years of Age, and since from time to time, I have had drawings in mind to reprove and testify against it, nor have I been altogether silent, altho' much discouraged by reason of it's being practiced by so many Friends, yea Elders too, and tho' I have formerly thought it strange, that the Church did not exclude it, by her discipline, and fix the Judgment of Truth upon it, yet now I am sensible such a thing is not easily done or accomplished, there being so strong opposition in many, that it cannot be brought to the Test, and Judgment brought forth into Victory in the cause at present, without danger of much strife and disorder in the Church, which is generally hurtful where-ever it prevaileth; therefore to be carefully avoided; however I hope we are all unanimous in our judgment, that whatever Friend hath anything from the movings of the Spirit of Truth to communicate to his Brethren, either by word or writing concerning this or any other matter, ought to be allowed and received in his Testimony, and borne with by his Brethren and Sisters, so long as they keep to the counsel and direction of the Holy Spirit, and therefore delivers nothing but what is according to Truth, altho' it happens to be never so contrary to the interest or inclinations of the Readers or Hearers.

Now I would such Friends as Practice or Plead for the above said Sin, Evil or Liberty, to consider solidly what Hardship they impose on such as are concern'd to bear Testimony against it; for while so many can reprove it, and give it that deserved Character, which is agreeable to it's nature, without implicitly condemning many of his Brethren, (Ministers and all say I, for they are the worst Enemies in this case the Church has to War with, or that Hell itself can procure in this case. This is very pinching, **B.L.** canst thou prove thy Allegations?) if not, what will become of thee? Never fear, Friend; Fear surprises, thou knows who; but the Truth is stronger than all the Powers of Hell. Blessed forever is the God of Truth, the Truth of God, the Truth which is God: So be it, saith my Soul.

Brethren and Sisters, as Transgressors in this Thing, which is very hard to do, yet if the Lord require such a Thing or Testimony of any Friend he is necessitated so to judge the Brethren and Sisters, or quench the Spirit in its Motions, in the Heart; for the case admits of no medium. Again I entreat those who slights and disregards the Testimony of any whom the Lord concerns to appear against this fleshly Liberty, to consider whom they oppose, and withstand. O! That I could prevail so far with all my dears Brethren and Sisters, that none would any more plead for or endeavor to defend the aforesaid unjust Practice; neither endeavor to shield it from the judgment of Truth.

No greater nor no better Law, say I, than to love God above all, and all our Fellow-Creatures as ourselves; these two contain Law, Prophets and Gospel, do to all as we would be done by. No greater Evil Hell can invent, than to profane and blaspheme the pure and Holy Truth, which is God all in all, and remove God's Creatures made after his own Image, from all the Comforts of Life, and their Country and procure for them, and bring them into all the miseries that Evil and Hypocrisy can procure and think of; these things are carried on by Christians, so called, and Ministers too, in the very greatest appearance of Sanctity in the whole World that ever I read or heard of; God which is the Truth, saith we shall not eat the cursed Fruit; our Ministers say we may eat, and lawfully too; which shall we believe?

We pretend not to love fighting with carnal Weapons, nor to carry Swords by our sides, but carry a worse thing in the Heart, as will I believe appear by and by; what, I pray and beseech you, dear Friends, by the tender Mercies of our God, to consider, can be greater Hypocrisy, and plainer contradiction, than for us as a People, to refuse to bear Arms, or to pay them that do, and yet purchase the Plunder, the Captives, for Slaves at a very great Price, thereby justifying their selling of them, and the War, by which they were or are obtained; nor doth this satisfy, but their Children also are kept in Slavery, *ad infinitum;* is not this plainly and substantially trampling the most Blessed and Glorious Testimony that ever was or ever will be in the World, under our Feet, and committing of Iniquity with, both Hands earnestly? Is this the way to convince the poor Slaves, or our Children, or Neighbours, or the World? Is it not the way rather to encourage and strengthen them in their infidelity, and their Hellish Practice of Fighting, Murdering, killing and Robbing one another, to the end of the World.

My dear Friends, I beg, I would entreat, in all humility, with all earnestness of mind, on the bended Knees of my Body and Soul; willingly and with all readiness, sincerely, if that would do, that you would turn t the Lord, the Blessed Truth, in your Hearts, for Direction, for Counsel and Advice; that you may quit your selves like Men, honourably of this so Hellish a Practice. Especially, you that have the Word of Reconciliation to preach to the Children of Men; and if you have any true tenderness of the Love of God in you, as I right well know, blessed be the Name of the Lord, all true Ministers have, you my dear Friends, consider weightily of these important concerns, and quit yourselves of yourselves and Slaves; for a good example in you might do a great deal of good, as a bad one will do, and has done a very great deal of mischief to the Truth; for the Eyes of the People are upon you, some for good, and some for Evil.

And my Friends, you that have Slaves, and do minister to others in our Meetings, consider, I entreat and beseech you concerning this thing in particular. What Burdens and Afflictions, Bondage, and sore Captivity you bring upon your dear and tender Friends, and keep them in, which cannot touch with this vile and hellish Practice, but are constrained to bear Testimony against it, as one of the greatest Sins in the World, all things considered: And against you too in some sort, as being in the practice yourselves, of that which is directly opposite to your own Pretensions, and a very great stumbling Block in the way of honest, godly Inquirers, which want Peace to their Souls.

What a great Strait these tender hearted mourning Souls must needs be in, think ye, betwixt Love and Duty; they love you dearly for the Truth's sake, and yet think it their Duty absolutely in the Fear and Love of God, to testify against the Sin, and you for continuing in it.

Dear Friends, what Peace can you have, in thus afflicting your Fellow Members; even the same Testimony they have with you in Meetings, where is the Blessed Unity and Fellowship, you have been preaching so many Years, as being sensible of one another's exercises, Bearers of one another's Burthens, having a deep sense and feeling of other's infirmities, or afflictions, or troubles.

What is become of this blessed experience, my Friends? Is it all left as to you, if, so, I must give my judgment, that you have not your constant dwelling in him, that was torched with a feeling of our infirmities, tempted in all cases like unto us, yet without Sin; and so are his Saints, for they are all of one, and they live with him; Night and Day, in his blessed Kingdom, which is within; and they love him dearly, they cannot avoid it, for he first loved them or us, and we cannot keep back our love from him any more than we can hinder, or stop the Rivers and Streams from running into the Ocean: For we having received all from him, of course all return or run to him again; it is the nature of his essence or divine being.

> What from Heaven is, to Heaven tends,
> That which descended, the same again ascends
> What from the Earth is, to Earth returns again,
> That which from Heaven is, the Earth cannot contain.

William Burling in his Preface, mentions something of the Lord's dealing with him, when he was about 10 or 12 Years of Age, which I suppose is about 50 Years ago, then there was much Discourse about many English and Dutch People, being taken into Turkey, or by the Turks into Slavery, and sold in the Market, for Term of Life, as Beasts in the Field. As our brave Christians so call'd do, and have done for many Years in Philadelphia, and elsewhere in America, by the poor Africans, which is ten times worse in us; all things considered; but what crying, wringing of Hands, what Mourning and Lamentations there was then by their Relations, Wives for their Husbands, Parents for their Children, Relations for their Friends, one Neighbour for another! What exclaiming against the Turk for his Tyranny and oppression, and cruel Dealing and Treatment, towards their Friends, and may be cursing and calling for Damnation to him and his God too.

Well my Friends, consider of it, and make an Application suitable to the circumstance of your own Slaves; for I do not believe in my Soul, the Turks are so cruel to their Slaves, as many Christians, so called, are to theirs, by what I have seen and heard of, in Barbados, and elsewhere; and I give you reason for it. I was near 18 Months, on board a large Vessel of 400 Tons in a Voyage in Scanderoon in Turkey, with four Men that had been 17 Years Slaves in Turkey, and I never did understand by them, that they were so badly used as the poor Africans are by some called Christians.

It is a very plain, parallel case, when our Spiritual Priests, under the Gospel of Christ will part with their slaves, no not for the Joy of the Lord. Then to be sure not for the comfort and Joy of their Brethren, and Sisters, who have been in sore Bondage, and Thraldom or Captivity, on that sinful Hellish Account, Slave-keeping, for 50 Years and more; and that by their Brethren and Sisters, which keeps them and will keep them, in spite of them, let them beg or pray, or say, or do what they can or will.

And all this while Preach, as their tender Friends do; who cannot touch with that sinful practice to gain the whole World; profess the same Pure Truth, Gospel, Unction, Anointing, Urim, and Thumim, Measure of the Spirit, pretend they have received the same Manifestation and Dispensation to preach, as their innocent Friends, Brethren,or Sisters have.

And really to give them their due, they come very near them in Words, for what I and some others can see; for we have observed them strictly as is our duty upon the Truths Account, which suffers so much by them, and their sinful practice, as well as their oppressed and greatly afflicted Brethren and Sisters.

I say these Guilty, come very near the Innocents in Words, except here and there, they do stretch and strain, rest, part, pervert, misconstrue, and misapply Scripture to serve their covetous Ends, or to justify and Practice, or to extenuate the Crime. If these things be done by them intentionally, we may say, without Breach of Charity. They shall receive the greater Damnation; as Christ himself said in a case almost as bad. (Matt. 23. 13-14)

Many worthy Men and Women have borne Testimony against this foul Sin, Slave-keeping, by Word and Writing; especially Ralph Sandiford, amongst many others, have writ excellently well, against that filthy Sin; far beyond what I can or do pretend to, being a Man of so very mean a capacity, and little Learning; but as I firmly believing it to be my duty, in the sight of God; I endeavor to do what I can and leave the Event to the Lord.

And as for any Slave-keepers, who are not impartial in the case; to say that Ralph Sandiford writ in a Spirit of Bitterness, or that he did not end his Life well. As to the first I have read his Book carefully, with Attention; and I do not remember a Word in it contrary to Truth, or any such sharp invectives, as may easily be found in Holy Scripture; altho' I have, it's true, because, I believe in my very Soul the cause does require it, for the nature of those Beasts, is in those Men, which do trade in Slaves; and much worse.

As to the second objection, that Ralph Sandiford did not end well; let such be entreated to remember the Men and Women of God, that were sent by the Lord. Ralph Sandiford had, and we now have, abundance of Old and Young pretended Prophet's, Prophets to lead us, poor Creatures, out of the way. And so they will many, unwary Souls; except the Lord our God be pleased to open our Eyes, to see the Hellish Darkness or Smoke, for whom the very Soul is grieved. God Almighty is my Witness. The 8th Month, 1736. *Benjamin Lay*.

Ralph Sandiford, above mentioned, was in great Perplexity of mind; ad having appreciation, which makes a wise man Mad, by which he was brought very low, with many Bodily Infirmities, long before he died; his Book largely set out, read it without partiality or prejudice, which is always blind, or very short sighted; and you may excellent weighty matters find in it; he was a very tender hearted Man before he came amongst Friends, as well as after, as I have heard from many honest Friends now living, that had much dealing, and intimate Conversation with him for many years. But before he died, by reason of his sore Affliction of mind, concerning Slave-keeping, as in his Book largely appear, and Infirmity of Body, he fell into a sort of Delirium: However I do believe if he had lived he would have overcome it; for I went to see him several times, a little before he died; I am not ashamed, nor afraid, to write it, altho' I be censured for it, as I have been with some others, for going to see him, altho' in Affliction, the only time for Visiting, as I humbly conceive, if we go in a right mind.

But O! Say the Slave-keepers, and must confess in their Hearts that Book *The Mystery of Iniquity,* as it is called, and titled; it tells Tales to the World, sets forth to the World's People, what a Parcel of Hypocrites, and Deceiver we are, under the greatest appearance and Pretentions to Religion and Sanctity that ever was in the World; we'll censure him, and his Book too, into the Bottomless Pit, if we can tho' we can't disprove a Word in it, for it's undeniable Truth, and so unanswerable; for we never understood, that any one ever attempted it, or so much as spoke of it; but that of that, Brethren and Sisters if it be sinful we are in the Iniquity, in the practice of Slave-keeping; and our Children by our means, encouragement, and appointment, not only so, but our Fathers and Mothers before us, in their generating Work; and some of them Ministers and Elders, with others of renown. They found the sweetness of it, and so do we, and we will continue in it; let who will or dare say nay; we'll condemn Ralph in his Grave, and his Book and all that favour it, or promote its being spread abroad, or being read, that exposes us, and we'll expose that, or especially him that writ it, by Slanders, and Surmises, and by insinuating all that ever we can hear or think of against him, now he is in his Grave; especially we did it before, but now more safely, for he can't contradict or oppose us now; so that if we can but render him odious in his Character, his Book will be invalidated in his Character, his Book will be invalidated in course with us that hate it, altho' we cannot disprove a tittle of it, especially with our Brethren and Sisters in strict Unity, in this Iniquity, and foulest of Sins, the African Trade.

It is true some may say, Christ in his great Love, hath forgiven Sins, committed in time of great Darkness and Ignorance; but if we should commit the grossest of evils now, in the clear light of this Gospel Day, continue in them, and plead for it too, we should withstand spiritual Moses, and our Damnation would be just.

We have been in this practice, that some poor Fellows, make such a stir about, above 50 Years; poor People which cannot purchase them, so pretend Conscience in the case, but let them that oppose our practice in Africans, bring those things upon us as above mentioned; if they can, then People may believe they are in the Right, and we in the Wrong. But let us consider by the way, Brethren and Sisters, if we go on arguing after this manner, some may be ready to object. But what shall we do, for People begin to see as clearly as when the Sun is in its Meridian Throne, young People as well as old, That this Practice of ours is as directly opposite to our holy Principles as Light is to Darkness, Christ to Belial, or God to Evil.

If the Case be thus, dear Brethren, as to be sure it is, how shall we stand our Ground? Our Ground, I say. It is true we may keep our Meeting Houses for a time, and we may join Forces with them that are in the Slave Practice; in strict Unity among ourselves, and with any other dear Friends of our own Mind, Relations, Customers, Chapmen, Workmen, or others that we can have any Influence over, Quakers or no Quakers, if they will but come to Meetings and do as we do, if not, say as we say, and plead for said sad Hell-Practice; or at least, Gentlemanlike, connive, palliate and dissemble to extenuate the Crime; and we will with all our Might, Interest and Strength, put forth, keep out, and hinder or prevent coming into our Synagogues, any that will oppose or condemn our Practice, or us for continuing in it. And further, as we have the Power of Discipline, our Ministers are forc'd , must of Necessity come to us for Certificates or Letters to recommend them, which we are very ready to give if they are fit for our Turn and Practice, and very good ones too. If they be but very poorly qualified in Words, and worse in Conduct and Life, yet they'll serve a small Turn. When he or she have got their Passport, one or other of us, a trusty Brother or Sister without Doors, will give them the Hint before they go forth, that if they should chance to meet, or go on purpose where they are to be found of heard of, any of the heavenly Party that is against our hellish Practice (or hellish Party that is against our heavenly Practice, for it is heavenly to us, it is Comfort and Joy to us, and we delight in it greatly and will keep in it) and may be. *My dear Friend, we will give thee a little Memorandum in thy Pocket of Places and Persons, which will be a great Help to thee poor dear Creature, thy dear Mind being so much exercised above other good Things that thou mayst chance to forget some other Matters though they be weighty: And wherever thou meets with any such as are above mention'd, when thee comes near their Dwellings, which thee may chance to hear of by strict Inquiry, inform Friends against them whatever thee can; tho' the Name of an Informer be odious, yet in some Cases it is thought necessary, as in this. But be sure when thou comes in thy Testimony, thresh 'em going, spare 'em not; and if an speak to thee after Meeting about it, say,* If the Coat fits thee, put it on; I had no Particular in View. This is and has been the Practice of many worthy Friends, so they hide themselves, and strengthen our Party bravely; so be it, say they.

Every good Tree bringeth good Fruit, but a corrupt Tree bringeth evil Fruit. (Matt. 7.17) Is there any eviler Fruit in the World than Slave-keeping? Anything more devilish? It is the very Nature of Hell itself, and is the Belly of Hell.

A good Tree cannot bring forth such cursed evil Fruit. (Matt. 7.18) as Slave trading, if this Practice be the worst, the greatest Sin in the World (with what goes and grows with it) as it is, to be sure. But if any should say that good Trees, good Men, may be in this Practice and encourage it, and if they may bring forth such Fruit, what Fruit must evil Trees bring forth. This will not hold a Parity of Reason; comparing Things with Things by an Equality, it will not hold good in any Case, much less in a religious Sense; there it is very odious, to be sure, and is very foul in Ministers especially. Let them keep on their Sheep's Clothing, and preach and pray as long as they may, until their Tongues are weary, and their Hearers Ears too; they'll preach more to Hell, I firmly believe, than they will to Heaven, while they continue in said Practice.

For Custom in Sin, hides, covers, as it were takes away the Gilt of Sin. Long Custom, the Conveniency of Slaves working for us, waiting and tending continually on us, beside the Washing, cleaning, scouring, cooking very nicely fine and curious, sewing, knitting, darning, almost ever at hand and Command; and in other Places milking, churning, Cheese-making, and all the Drudgery in Dairy and Kitchen, within doors and without. And the proud, dainty, lazy Daughters and Sons sit with their hands before 'em, like some of the worst idle Sort, and if they want a Trifle, rather than rise from their Seats, call the poor Slave from her Drudgery to come and wait upon them. These Things have been the utter Ruin of more than a few; and yet encouraged by their own Parents, for whom my Spirit is grieved, some of which were and are Preachers in great Repute, as well as others.

Now, dear Friends, behold a Mystery! These Ministers that be Slave-keepers, and are in such very great Repute, such eminent Preachers, given to Hospitality, charitable to the Poor, loving to their Neighbours, just in their Dealings, temperate I their Lives, visiting of the Sick, sympathizing with the Afflicted in Body or Mind, very religious seemingly, and extraordinary devout and demure, and in short strictly exact in all their Decorums, except Slave-keeping, these, these, be the Men and Women for the Devil's purpose, and are the choicest Treasure Evil can or has to bring out to establish Slave-keeping. These are the very Men, or People of both Sexes, that come the nearest the Scribes and Pharisees of any People in the whole World, if not sincere: For the Scribes are exact and demure seemingly in their Appearance before Men, according to Christ's Account of them, and yet the worst Enemies the deart Lamb had. And I do surely believe that one such as these, now in this our Day, in this very Country, does more disservice and Hurt in the Church, in Slave-keeping, than twenty Publicans and Prostitutes: For by their extraordinary Conduct, in Hypocrisy, smooth and plausible appearance, they draw into the Snare almost insensibly, and so beguile unstable Souls before they are aware, which is sorrowful to consider as well as write, their Example being much more powerful than others.

And Friends, that concerning the delicate Damsels, or fine idle Dames, it may be pretty much like it with the young Men, and may be the old ones, that have their Slaves to low, sow, thresh, winnow, split Rails, cut Wood, clear Land, make Ditches and Fences, fodder Cattle, run and fetch up the Horses, or fine curious pacing Mares, for young Madam and Sir to ride about on, impudently and proudly gossiping from House to House stuffing their lazy ungodly Bellies.

Then old Sir Master calls, "Slave, fetch my best Gelding quickly, for me to ride to Meeting to preach the Gospel of glad Tidings to all People, and Liberty to the Captives, and opening the Prison-Doors to them that are bound; but I'll keep thee in Bondage nevertheless, help thy self if thee can. I charge thee to work very hard when I am gone, and before be very ready to wait on me and my Children when we come home, if they come with me, or else wait till they do come, and then take their Horses, and look well after them; and then make haste in, all of ye, and be ready to wait upon us, and keep good Fires above stairs or below, and mind your Business well, or I'll take a Corse with you; don't think that I'll give 70 or 80 Pounds apiece for you, for nothing but to lie lazing about like Gentlemen, doing nothing, you shall work now you are young, for when you are very old, you will not do much, I suppose, and then you must be maintained, you and your Wives and Children and Children's Children; and if you do not behave yourselves well, you'll be but badly provided for, I believe, when you are past your Labour, whatever you are now."

Dear Friends, these Things are true in Fact, and have been the ruin of many, Body and Soul, and will be of more I greatly fear; beside and above all, the Evil it brings upon the pure, blessed, unchangeable TRUTH.

And my dear, my very dear Friends, I must say, I must say, and it is the Experience and certain Knowledge of my own Soul, that except People will be willing to come to a Separation, a Separation, a Separation:

From this Thing, to wit, Slave Practice, they never can nor will see the Evil of it, as it really is in itself.

I say my own Experience when I lived in Barbados about 18 Years ago, where we had much Business in Trading, and the poor Slaves would come to our Shop and Store, hunger-starv'd, almost ready to perish with Hunger and Sickness, great Numbers of them would come to trade with us, for they seemed to love and admire us, we being pretty much alike in Stature and otherways; and my dear Wife would often be giving them something for the Mouth, which was very engaging you that read this may be sure, in their deplorable Condition Oh! My Soul mourns in contemplating their miserable, forlorn, wretched State and Condition that mine Eyes beheld them in then, and it is the same now, and will remain except the great almighty Being, either immediately or instrumentally shall be pleased to put a Stop to it; for they are yearly by Shiploads poured in upon, and received by the People, many Thousands in one Year, Year after Year, as thought, up and down America, besides what vast Numbers area increased by

Generation daily. O Lord God Almighty, where will this Practice lead us that are called thy People, Dearest God, and make so great a Profession of being lead and guided by thy eternal Spirit, which is the glorious Truth unchangeable and precious, and without End. But I trust, dearest One, thou wilt be pleased to stop and end this Practice, that is more like Hell than Heaven, to be sure.

I having made a little Digression, may resume the Matter relating to my dear Wife, and the Slaves. She was a tender-hearted Woman, and, as I said, would be very often giving them something or other; Biscuits which sometimes we had in abundance, Cheese, Meat and Fish which we had plenty of in that Country; so my dear sweet Sarah, she would hand it to them, here and there to those that she thought wanted it most, tho' all wanted enough, God Almighty knows.

Here and there a favourite Slave, may be kept by the Slave-master for the Slave-master's Glory and Pride to wait on them, amongst their proud, lazy, dainty, tyrannical, gluttonous, drunken, debauched Visitors, the Scum of the infernal Pit, a little worse than the same that comes of Grease, Dirt, Dung, and other Filthiness, as, it may be Limbs, Bowels and Excrements of the poor Slaves, and Beasts, and other Matters, but this I say serves to make Rum of, and Molasses, for that is the Use it is put to, with other Ingredients pretty much like it; and these People in the Islands may laugh at us for being ridiculously infatuated, to send away our excellent good Provisions, and other good Things, to purchase such filthy Stuff, which tends to the Corruption of Mankind, and may be send their broken Slaves along with their Rum, to complete the Tragedy, that is to say, to destroy the People in Pennsylvania, and ruin the Country.

Dear Friends, or any of my Fellow-creatures, I must confess I am apt to digress, but when such dangerous Filthiness comes in my Way, I think it my Duty to make it appear if possible to others; for it is so to me, exceeding sinful above Measure, I will assure you, more than what I can speak or write abundantly; if it should be so to you, I hope you will endeavor to avoid it, and pray for Heaven's Assistance, without which all is nothing.

As to what was touched on before, when my dear Sarah had given to them what she thought fit within-doors, we have taken some more of the same sort and put it into the Street. The poor Creatures would come running, and tearing, and rending one another, to get a part in the scramble their poor Bellies were so empty, and so ravenous were they, that I never saw a parcel of Dogs more eager about meat than they always were. This Scramble was commonly on a First Day, before we went to Meeting, which was their Market-day as well as the Slave's Hallowing-Day, when they are exempted from their Labour, they come down to Town, many Hundreds of them, they that could get or steal any Thing, a little Sugar, or Cotton, Ginger, Aloes, Rum, Cocoa-Nuts, Pine-Apples, Oranges, Lemons, Citrons, Old Iron, Wood for Fire, steal any Thing out of Houses, Yards, or anywhere, or any Thing that was not too hot or too heavy, and bring it to Market, on Sunday as they call it, to get a penny or something for the Mouth and they that could not get any ting to bring to Market, they could come to Town if possibly they could hold out and keep from falling down and fainting by the Way, they would come to Town if possibly they could hold out and keep from falling being perished with Hunger and hard Labour the Week before; I say these poor Slaves could get no Truck in the Country to bring to Market, yet they would if possible come to Town, and see what they could beg or steal there. (Who can blame them if it was ten times worse, they being under such unmerciful Tyrants.) These poor Slaves being in Town in this miserable Condition, with not a Crumb of good or bad to put into their Mouths, ready to drop as they walked or crawled along the Streets, many of them hearing of us, for we were very much known amongst them, would come to our Door, if they came before we were gone to Meeting, they would stand as thick as Bees, and I may say their Appearance was dismal enough to move a very hard Heart; so we used to give them a little of something at Times, as we found some Freedom, considering our Circumstances; but if we gave to some, and did not to all, as to be sure we could not, oh how the poor Creatures would look. I say many Hundreds would come and flock about us; and them that receiv'd, O how thankful, with bended Knees; but them that did not, what Words can set forth the dejected sinking Looks that appeared in their Countenances. Shall I ever forget them?

Many of these poor Creatures, in Town and Country, were sent to Market by their Masters or

Mistresses, at other Times, and they would come to us to lay out their Money, if we had such Goods as they wanted, and when they came in, seem'd to rejoice to see us together,, we were so very much alike; and would lift up their Hands with Admiration, and say, "That little backararar man, (for so they call white People) go all over world to look for that backarar woman for himself." But we, alas! Are parted! Dear Sarah has died!

Here Friends you may see and understand the powerful Influence long Custom, Conveniency, Intimacy, and Profit has to insinuate itself into our Affections; for I have often heard my dear Wife say in her Life-time, and express the Danger she was in when living in Barbados, of being leavened into the very Nature of the Inhabitants, Pride and Oppression: So my dear Sarah, seeing the Evil and the Danger, was willing and desirous to leave the Island, and indeed so was I.

But, my Friends, here I must come to that that is not very agreeable to Flesh and Blood, which is Confession of Sins: For although I never was Owner of a Slave myself, and all Friends in Barbados could never persuade me to purchase one, I humbly bless the Lord my good God for that and this is now my Comfort and dear Joy and sweet Experience: Yet I must confess, and I have not full Peace without it, yet I may say I have been sorely grieved to see and hear the inexpressible Cruelty, Torture, and Misery, these poor Wretches were and are put to, Night and Day, yet although, as I have said, I saw and heard of such very great Barbarity used toward the Slaves, Night and Day, yet for want of dwelling near enough to the blessed Truth, I was leavened too much into the Nature of the People there which are Masters and Mistresses of Slaves, though I never had nor would have any of my own, but by conversing, trading, and living daily amongst them, were there is vast Numbers, abundance coming daily to buy Goods and to beg, some to steal, we had abundance stolen from us at Times, the worth of ten, fifteen, or near twenty Shillings at a time, come into the Shop whole Droves together, lay the Scheme I suppose, come by Appointment; when many are come in they seem in great haste, one would say, Serve me, another, Serve me, serve me; come sometimes by twilight and within Night, then was their Time; so when we were in a hurry, one would run away with one Thing, another with another, and so on. Very much we lost to be sure. Sometimes I could catch them, and then I would give them Stripes sometimes, but I have been sorry for it many times, and it does grieve me to this Day, considering the extreme Cruelty and Misery they always live under. Oh my Heart has been pained within me many times, to see and hear; and no, now, now, it is so.

Shall we fetch and steal them out of their own Country, where God Almighty has made them and placed them, and in taking of them murder many, very many, and serve them that we take alive ten times worse; steal Husband from Wife, Wife from Husband; steal the Children from their Parents, bring them here or elsewhere amongst our extraordinary Christians, worse Thieves than the others by far; they work 'em, whip and starve 'em almost to death, and if the poor Slave steal a little to satisfy Hunger, he is tormented without Mercy. Be these Christians, and Ministers too, that encourage and plead for these Things? It must be all a Lie, and that is of the Devil, *for when he speaketh a Lie, it is of himself.* (John 8. 44) I do believe in my Soul, if Christ was here in that very Body, he would say as much to some Quakers as he said to the Scribes and the Pharisees. If the Devil be a Murderer and a Liar, what are our Slave-Merchants? What does our dear Slaves with their Slaves think of these Things? Can a good Tree bear Slave-Trading for Gain? Not many Slave keepers bring forth Fruit to Perfection. I am much afraid Slave keeping will bring forth Fruits to the Death.

> Some queries: Are not Slave keepers the Servants of Sin? Are our Slave keepers ashamed of their Sin? Are our Slave keepers free from Sin? Are Slave keepers able to convince the Gainsayers? Are not Slave keepers of the Circumcision, unruly vain Talkers? Do not Slave keepers subvert whole Houses, for filthy Lucre? Are not Slave keepers Liars? Don't they deserve to be rebuked sharply, as being very unsound in the Faith? Don't these give way to Fables, and turn from the Truth? What think ye, my Brethren and Sisters? Unto the Pure all things are pure; if literally, then Robbing and Killing, as well as Slave keeping. Do not these deny God in works and yet pretend to know him? Have these Men sound Doctrine, Gravity and Sincerity? Have not these Men of the contrary Part need to be ashamed, when we have so many evil things to say of them, and very justly too? Do these adorn the Doctrine of God our Saviour with Slave keeping?

But, my Friends, you that practice Tyranny and Oppression for Slave keeping is such; he that assumes in arbitrary Manner, unjustly, Dominion over his

Fellow-Creature's Liberty and Property, contrary to Law, Reason or Equity, He is a wicked sinful Tyrant, guilty of Oppression and great Iniquity: But he that trades in Slaves and the Souls of Men, does so; therefore--- Beside Friends, the very Name of a Tyrant is odious, to God, to good Men, yea to bad Men too; and the Nature and Practice is much worse.

And Friends, you that follow this forlorn filthy Practice, do you not consider that you are opening a Door to others, or setting them an Example to do the like by you, whenever it shall please the Almighty to suffer them to have Power over us, as a Scourge to us for our Sins, what Reason then shall we have to complain? If any of you ever read the History of the English Slaves in Algiers, how would you like that yourselves? There was some Discourse of its being printed in Philadelphia: I with it might, for the sake of some.

My dear Wife has often spoke of a Passage in or near Spike's in Barbados; going hastily into a very plain-coat outside Friend's House, there hung up a Slave stark naked, trembling and shivering, with such a Flood of Blood under him that so surprised the little Woman she could scarce contain; but at last a little recovering, she says to some in the Family, "What's here to do?" They began exclaiming against the poor miserable Creature, for absconding a day or two, may be by reason of his cruel Usage, as by this Barbarity we may imagine.

Another Piece of Barbarity, of one Richard Parrot a Cooper, which I knew; he used to whip his Slaves on Second-day Mornings very severely, to keep them in awe. It is usual for these miserable Slaves to get together on First Days, to bewail and lament their forlorn Condition that they are in one to another. One says, "My Master very bad Man"; another, "My Mistress very bad Woman". This Parrot's Slave, a lusty Fellow, a Cooper, and used to get his Master 7 shillings 6 pence a day, being valued at 100 pounds or more; he says, "My Master Parrot very bad Man indeed, whips, whips poor Slaves every Monday Morning for nothing till me no bear no longer". This was while we lived in Barbados. I knew Parrot very well, having been at his House; and abundance more of such like Things while we visited there.

1736, the 29th of the 8th Month, this Morning between 2 & 3 this was written.

It arose in my Mind in Love of Truth, that as the blessed immaculate Lamb was said to be full of Grace, and full of Truth; s Slave-keeping and trading is of the Devil, full of all Ungraciousness and all Untruth. The True Child and Heir of Hell, the begotten of Evil, indeed, but not in Truth nor any part of it. So may many of our Ministers say to the Slave-traders and Keepers: We have been begotten thro' Evil, by our Example and Pleading for it, and by our Condemning and Disowning many worthy Friends, of innocent Lives, for testifying against Slavery and against us for living and continuing in it; but we will do it for all that. What do we care for their Testimony? Shall, we, our Wives, or Sons, or Daughters, when our Fellow-Merchants come to visit us, run to wait on them, their Horses, their Chariots and Equipage, Cooking, Sculling and waiting? No, we despise it, and them that do it.

We may safely say, without Breach of Charity that there is a Lying Spirit in the Mouths of all them that keep or trade in Slaves, and say it is lawful in this blessed Gospel Day; let them pretend to what they will or may; whether Hearers of Prophets, or Preachers, although there be or should be four hundred or four hundred thousand of them, no matter for their great Number, the Truth is over them all; although them that are and were out of the Truth have fallen, and may fall, by their Means, by their lying Persuasions and lying Practice; I say their great and lying Pretensions have and may and will cause many more, I fear, to fall, as well as the other false Prophets did. It is enough to make one tremble to think what will become of those Prophets that prophesy Lies in the Name of the Lord, and teach the People to keep Slaves in this pure Gospel Day; it has and does cause the Eyes of many dear Servants and Handmaids amongst us to run down with Tears, because of this sinful Practice.

I can truly say, I have had large and long Experience since I came into America, that many of our Ministers and Elders are not only in the Bond of Iniquity, but also in the Gall of Bitterness. Do but reprove for these Things (Slave-Practice) and they will, if possible put you into the Stocks, with or in the high Gate or some other way, even though dwelling near or in the House of the Lord. Is it not enough almost to break ones Heart, to see this Practice of Slavery lived in and pleaded for by our Preachers and

Elders? My dear and tender Friends, Should we or shall we always hearken unto the Voice or Words of false Prophets that teach lies in the Name of the Lord. Then what a Root of Gall and Wormwood appears in these Slave-Keepers when they are reproved, Ministers especially, to my certain knowledge, and long experience. What shall we do, Dear Friends, if the Lord should entirely hide his Face from us, because of this Slave-Keeping, and from others almost as bad.

Though this wickedness Slave-Keeping, be sweet in the Mouth, they can salve it with smooth Words, yet Torment is under the Tongue. Yet inwardly, the Slave-Keeper, by his pleasant Gain, gotten by his Slaves, and swallowed down, will bite as bad as the Gall of Asps and Vipers if not repented of and forsaken before Death; for when Death approaches, Sin will sting. You that keep Slaves, your covenant with Death, and Hell shall be broken when their Wine, their Pleasures, and Profit, gotten by Slave-Keeping, will be as Poison and the cruel Venom of Asps, in the end, or I am mistaken. The Slave Trading Preachers break the greatest Commandment and teach others so to do. I believe these they say will sometimes in Meetings, and do ill in Slave Trading; will come far behind Publicans and Prostitutes.

9th Month, 1736, as I sat in Concord Meeting House, it was their Quarterly Meeting; I may say it was a sweet and comfortable time to me; it came into and arose in my mind, in Love of Truth, that if our Slave-Keepers had been, or now would be faithful to God, the Truth, and would bring up their Slave to some Learning, Reading and Writing, and endeavour to the utmost of their power in the sweet Love of Truth to instruct and teach 'em the principles of truth and righteousness, and teach them some Honest Trade or Employment, and then set them free; and all the time Friends are teaching of them let them know that they intend to let them go free in a very reasonable time: and that our Religious Principle will not allow of such Severity, as to keep them in everlasting Bondage and Slavery.

This might according to my way of thinking, beget such Love and Tenderness in them, toward their Masters or Mistresses, and to the blessed Truth for their Sakes; that it might be a means to convince some of them.

And should they come to receive the pure Truth, in the Love of it; as, blessed be the Lord, many of us have, and in that sweet Love, which is constraining, come under concern and necessity, to go and visit their Brethren, of their own colour, and Country, and Language, and preach the Gospel of eternal Salvation unto them, from Sin and Captivity, both of Body and Soul, this would be a glorious work indeed, and well worth our Friend's pains, charge and time, that they might spend about it; and the best compensation to God and Man, as I think, that they can possibly make, for being so long in a practice that has so much Wickedness attending of it continually.

The many Hundreds of Thousands, that are now in Slavery, were they at Liberty, as we are, had the same Education, Learning, Conversation, Books, sweet Communion in our Religious Assemblies; I believe many of them would exceed many of their Tyrant Masters in Piety, Virtue and Godliness; and their bright Genius, which I know they have, would be in livened; for I have conversed with many of them, for Liberty is Life, and Slavery is Death, nay the very thoughts of it to a right thinking Animal, as Man or Woman.

Is this *preaching glad tidings to the meek,* as many of them are and *bind up the broken hearted; to proclaim Liberty to the Captives, and opening of the Prison, to them that are bound;* (Isaiah 61.1) and yet keep them in double Bondage, Body and Soul, them and theirs for ever more. If there be greater contradiction under the Sun; many dear and tender Friends are mistaken, as well as myself. But how do Slave Merchants *proclaim the acceptable Year of the Lord?* (Isaiah 61.2) to their Slaves the Day of Vengeance they mean, and a long Day it is; but I believe the Lord will repay it, tho' he suffers it long: But I pray and beseech you; you hard-hearted Ministers, of all persuasions in Church and State, that are Christians; how do you comfort all that mourn, and are in Misery, as great for aught I can learn as any that be under oppression by the very worst persons in the known World.

But my dear and tender Friends, how does this cruelty and partiality agree with our principles as a People, which have been preaching up Perfection in holiness of Life: for near a Hundred Years and the universal Love of God to all People, of all colours and Countries, without respect of Persons: Have we forgot this blessed Testimony for which our dear Friends suffered in Old and New England.

The 2d of the 9th Month 1736. If Two Weeks Meeting had had anything material against me, or Monthly Meeting; they should have appeal'd to Quarterly Meeting before we came away. But some Friends have been the Instruments of the Death of my Dear Wife I believe. Hath it not been the Practice of the Guilty in all Ages, to lay Traps and Snares, to entangle and ensnare the Innocent? Did you not do so, two or three of you, of the Monthly Meetings, at the Quarterly Meetings, Yearly Meetings at Philadelphia and Burlington; when I insisted of having the Letter from Colchester read, did not you strenuously insist, that I should consent that then the matter should be concluded in that Meeting so to go no further; and you had got a strong Party there the same time, to conclude the Business, according to your own minds; is not this laying a Snare? In the same Meeting accusing me falsely for seeking a Party to deter, any from speaking their Minds; and opposed and hindered me from reading a Letter or two from Colchester; which you knew you did not like to hear, because they would have confirmed our Certificate more fully. How did William Penn and William Mead, at their trial, in the Old Baily, London, like such arbitrary Proceedings, as well as many, yea very many more of our Dear and Worthy Friends and Elders, in the beginning, before and by wicked unjust Judges, in Old England and New England too, in particular, as the *Book of Sufferings* largely sets forth.

How many profuse, profligate Creatures, have come in Servants to this Country, which have been stated not only as Members, but Ministers in full Unity, in less time than I have been here; is it not intolerable then, that three or four Men, Slave Keepers, have the whole Rule of Discipline, and Govern contrary to all Justice and Equity. Time for such old rusty Candlesticks to be moved out of their Places, who have disowned many less Guilty then themselves; if it is not so now, who will make me a Liar.

Abington, The 11th of 9th Month 1736. I suppose the pure holy eternal Being, which made of one Blood all Nations of Men and Women to dwell upon the face of the Earth, did not make others to be Slaves to us, any more than we to be so to them; if God has appointed the Bounds of their Habitations, what Man fearing God, dare to remove or receive them when they are removed.

How would many Dear Friends like to be banished from their Native Countries, from Wives, Children and Friends, although but for a few Years, both from Old and New England especially? Are all these Things forgotten by us, and a thousand times more; are the Progeny in this Age, doing the same Things themselves which their Progenitors so greatly complained of, and justly too; but this Progeny have been and are acting a Thousand times worse, and more cruelly; for our dear and worthy Friends and Progenitors were Banished from England but for a few Years, and where they might and did Preach and help forward the Gospel of Christ; but the poor Slaves and their Progeny, have been Stolen, Banished, Tortured and Tormented, for ever more; to the great and unutterable hindrance of the Blessed Gospel of Peace and Salvation, for which our dear Progenitors, suffered so deeply by their Persecutors.

And this now is carried on, encouraged and done by them, that profess to be led by the same pure Holy Spirit, as their Progenitors were.

But my dear and tender Friends, you that are clear of this vile practice, I pray and beseech you, especially that you keep so, and have no Fellowship with such unfruitful Works of Darkness but rather, I say, rather reprove them, as being worthy, wherever you come, for the Lord, the Truth's sake.

The 22d of the 9th Month. When I have mildly reasoned with some Friends concerning their Hostility, in Carrying this Friend, out of Meetings so often, and keeping him out by Constable and other ways; as at Philadelphia, Burlington and Concord, etc. without so much as pretending they have used any Gospel Order with him, in any Monthly or Quarterly Meeting, as a disorderly Person.

O but, say some, he is a very troublesome Person, and has been so for many Years; and is too censorious about Trading I Slaves, or against Traders in, and Keepers of Slaves; and positively affirms, that no Man or Woman, Lad or Lass ought to be suffered, to pretend to Preach Truth in our Meetings, while they live in that Practice; which is all a Lie.

And further, he boldly affirms, that no Person whatsoever has any Right, or ought according to

Truth's Discipline, to be suffered to have the Rule and Government, or any Part of it, in the Church of God, which is the Kingdom of God, while he himself is in League with Evil, and is managing the affairs of the Kingdom, which Slave Trading is, as has been proved.

But some that have not, and will not keep Slaves of their own, may say, we must not be too censorious, for we are often at their Houses, and Eat and Drink with satisfaction, and have their Slaves to wait on us, our Horses, Wives and Children. Beside all these Things, we buy, sell, Trade, get Gain by and with them, we must be careful how we offend our Benefactors. Dear Friends here is yet a stronger Factor than the other so in Pleasure and Profit, we love to participate with their Offspring, so they be but Rich; for many of us have joined Affinity with thee Oppressors for Gains, by marrying with their rich Children, and if we become Prophets, and can prophesy such things as they like, so we are badly favoured. The Scriptures speak especially to our Brethren in their great Iniquity they do to their Slaves, up and down in the World, and their Offspring, always repeated and repeating for evermore, with all the Torture and Torments that Evil can invent or devise, with all their Accomplices.

But although some of us, that are Slave Masters and Traders, do allow that the beginning of this Practice was of Evil, and that these Instruments are now carrying of it on very powerfully, and as it had a beginning in Evil, so it must have an End.

One time, when I was reasoning with an eminent Preacher R.J. at his House in Philadelphia, concerning Slave-keeping, which has defied the living God so many Years, and still continues so to do. He, the said R.J., was pleased then and there to tell me, that I loved the Slaves better than I did my Friends; and accused me at Stephen Jenkin's House, before many Witnesses, of being the Death of my Dear Wife, and a Persecutor of the Church; but before that I charged him with being instrumental of separating my Dear Wife from me by Death, in Writing for a separate Certificate for my Wife, to a Meeting to which we never did belong, as if he and two or three more had a mind to separate us; which is now brought to pass.

The great Judge of Heaven and Earth, may be pleased to forgive them, I hope I shall in time. These things must be borne with I suppose, and more; when I have said to some Friends, Slave-keepers and their Adherents, that it seemed a little strange or novel, that a Friend should be hurried out of Meetings so constantly and roughly, before he be disowned or some way dealt with for some disorder or other, contrary to the known and acknowledged discipline of Friends as a People.

If thy Brother is overtaken in a Fault, go to him and tell him his fault, between him and thee; if he hears thee thou has gained thy Brother; if he will not hear thee, then take two or three with thee; if he will not hear them, then take them to the Church; and if he will not hear the Church, then, not till then, cast him forth. (Reference: Matthew 18.15-20)

My Dear Friends, have any of these things been done to Benjamin Lay and yet still continue to cast him out, cast him out, cast him out, he is a trouble-some Fellow, and has been so for many Years. Did our dear and well beloved Friends in Boston 60 or 70 Years ago, think this a just way of Proceeding, to be taken into Custody, put in Jail, Whipt severely, Banished from the Town, time after time, without any legal Proceedings, only for being obstinate Quakers, as they were pleased to call them; dare to come again when they had Whipped them out of the Town so often. When I have put some Friends in mind of this, concerning our Dear Tender Friend's great Suffering in New England, in a Book called *New England Judged,* some Friends have answered cautiously but this of Friends Suffering in Boston is true, for I have been upon the Spot or Lot of Ground, where the Dear Lambs were put to Death (on Boston Common); for the Word of God and the Testimony of Jesus Christ, the Truth.

It has been so that the very best of Men and Women and Instruments that ever were in the World, though they had been never so much enlightened or illuminated from on High; they grow dark again, as they go from the Light, from God, from Truth, which are one in Nature and Essence, although three Names, for Men as Men do know that have good Natural Eyes, that the further they go from the Light outwardly, the more they go into Darkness until at length they cannot see anything clearly, or at last not at all; and this comes upon Men because they love Darkness and they live in Darkness and walk in Darkness, and at last Darkness in Sin seems to be Light unto them. This is a dreadful State indeed: O that it may appear so before it be too late, to some poor Souls, is my true Desire for their eternal Welfare which I desire as for my own Soul.

A Saint in Light, or an enlightened Saint, the same put the Primitive Saints in Mind. You keep them in a watchful frame of Mind; you that were once in Darkness, are not Light, in the Light or in the Lord, the same bids them walk as the Children of the Light, and of the Day, which is Light, and to walk and work in as well as to live and dwell in this the New Jerusalem, the Church of the first or true Born with God, the Light in Heaven, whose Gates are always open to Saints in Light, no Night, no Darkness there, no need of Sun, Moon, Stars, Candles or Lamps, for the Lord God, the Lamb, the Truth, the Light, is or are the Light forevermore. *Benjamin Lay*

And so is the Heavenly Food for Saints to feed of freely; this is the Tree of Life (Revelation 22), which bears twelve Manner of Fruit, and yields her Fruit every Month, always ready, always ripe, fresh, green, pure and lovely to behold, sweet and delicious to the Saint's taste, to them that are clean, that have been cleansed by the Light, by the Life of the Lamb, which follows him through many Tribulations, wherever he goes and leads them until he brings them into the Green Pastures of Life beside the still Waters of Life, of Comfort indeed, the pure River of Water of Life, which is with God, and is God living in sanctified Hearts.

O let the Inhabitants of the Tree, the River, the Rock, Sing aloud for Joy; from henceforth for evermore: So be it, Glory, Glory, endless to the All in All faith in my Soul. *Benjamin Lay*

The 27th of the 9th Month 1736. This is Written in pure Love, concerning the Pure in Heart, of all Colours and Countries in the whole World; these are the Dwellers in the Rock of Ages.

Abington, The 7th Month, 1736. My Dear and Well beloved Friends; my Joy and the Crown of all my sweet Delights in this World, I can truly say, is the true Unity with my true Brethren, which are the true Church in God the Father, and he in them, ever reigning in his own Blessed Kingdom, Body, House, Tabernacle, New Jerusalem, or a Tent, synonymous Terms; no Divination could prevail, or enchantments against 'em; but when our Dear Friends, went to look at, and long after the Pleasures, Pride, Profit and Friendship of this World, then they came to be snared with this cursed Sin, Slave-Trading, as well as some other gross Sins, of which this is Chief, considering the Hellish Train of Filthiness, which has, does, and ever will attend it, and is inseparable from it; for it is granted by all sober wise Men and Women that truly fear God, and dearly love the Truth in Sincerity, and are well acquainted with this foul Trade from the beginning, and in all its progressions to this Day; I say such as have had a true Account, do know that those that are employed in this Trade, are some of the worst of Men, and withal some of the worst of Thieves, Pirates and Murderers, from whence our lesser Pirates have proceeded. And many of these lesser Pirates have been punished with Death, and some other ways; but the much greater Villains by far, not only go free but are encouraged, and have been near 50 Years, if not more, by us as a People, by buying of their cursed Hellish-gotten Ware, at a very great Price. And all this Time pretending to the most holy pure Religion in the whole World, to do unto all, as we would they should do unto us, and as we find in Scripture *to visit the Fatherless, and Widows, in their Afflictions, and keep ourselves unspotted from the World;* (James 1. 27) but I know no worse Evil to make to Widows and Fatherless Children, and to bring into Affliction and Bondage, and sore Captivity indeed, than this Hellish practice Pennsylvania, Slave-Keeping.

But these Hellish Miscreants, these Men-Stealers, pretend they fetch away these poor Creatures, that they may not kill one the other, when they are the Murderers which sets 'em to the Work, (a cursed work it is) for as I have had an Account, near 35 Years ago, when 10 or 12 Sail of Vessels come on the Coast of Guinea, and they cannot catch Slaves enough to Freight their Vessels by the Seaside, and in Rivers where they send their Boats in Search and Pursuit of them, where they are acquainted; for they being used to the Business know where to go; and to find out some old Africans that they have been used to trade with, which will bring off in Canoes, their Wives or Children, or their Neighbours Wives, and Children if they can catch 'em in Woods, or anywhere else, so bring 'em and sell them to our brave Christians, which come there with Ships for that purpose. O brave! Give 30 shillings for an African and sell him for 30 pounds or 40, 50 or 60 70, 80, 90, 100 pounds or more: Who would but be a Trader in Slaves and Souls of Men, altho' he goes to Hell for it, and in the meantime entail an Iniquity on his own, and his

Neighbour's Posterity to their Destruction and the Ruin of the whole Country beside.

Above 30 Years ago, when I was a common Sailor, I had this Account, and likewise by some Sailors on Board Captain Reeves, coming this Voyage to Philadelphia, who had been at Guinea, and I suppose they had been Pirates.

These vile Fellows on Board Captain Reeves, in their Drink used to tell what cursed Work their former Captain and Sailors made with the poor Africans in their Passage, for their Lusts; the Captain 6 or 10 of 'em in the Cabin, and the Sailors as many as they pleased; with much more too foul for me to mention, or for chaste Ears to hear.

But I pray, I beg, and beseech you my Friends, in the pure Love and Fear of God; consider what part have true Believers with such unbelievers we can never reconcile Slave Keeping with our Principles. Now my dear Friends, let us consider the matter a little further, concerning these Men Stealers, and weigh it in the Balance of the Sanctuary, which is Equity and Justice. Consider I say, the different circumstances of times and things; it may be these wicked Creatures have been unhappily brought up most of their Lifetime; my Soul pities them on that Account; had they had that good Education, Conversation, Books and Mutual Love, in Holy Illuminations, sweet Communion together in our solemn Meetings and Gatherings together, and the Heavenly Showers which many times, yea very often and frequent to my sure and certain Knowledge, and to the great mutual sweet and heavenly Comfort of my poor Soul, with many more of my dear Friends; I say the many Heavenly Showers that have dropped as the Dew, and distilled as the small Rain, in our tender Souls immediately, many times, yea innumerable, and instrumentally, by the Blessed Messengers of Peace and Salvation, which were sent by the high and lofty one, that inhabiteth eternity and dwelleth in Light, who had a tender regard, Blessed by his Holy Name, to those Poor Men and Women too, that were Poor indeed, and truly contrited, and sat trembling before his Divine and Glorious Majesty. They are ready to receive him that was and is the Word that made all things. When they had received him, that or we, We were made to rejoice with Joy unspeakable, being filled with him that was, and is, and ever will be the Glory and true rejoicing of his People, and dear Children, all the World over; can appeal to him that knows all Things. They love him more than all things here below, yea than their natural Lives.

Shall we, I say as People who have been Blessed with so great Privileges, and high Favours, forsake the Holy Commandment of Loving Truth above all, and turn to worship for covetous ends, the worst Idol that ever Evil set up in the World.

Sure those wicked Men above mentioned will rise up in Judgment against us; for had they been so highly favoured in all respect, as Friends as a People have been, who knows but they might have been as great Saints as any in the Church of Christ at this Day; for had Friends stood faithful in their Testimony against this Practice from the beginning they might have convinced many, and stopt 'em in their career;

but now they may say, and that truly too, we have been a means to encourage and strengthen them in their wicked ways; for when they brought in a Cargo of Slaves, there were those ready to purchase them, and at a great Price. Well my dear and tender Friends, although I touch thus close to ease my afflicted mind, which has been tossed as with a Tempest at times, above 17 Years, on this sad Account Slave Keeping, yet I write not this of all by no means, I know and believe there are many Friends, that dare not touch it, for any Profit whatsoever. I do hope there are some Thousands will not bow the Knee to this Slavery. It has been said, that all do not see it so great a Sin as I and some others make it; and for that reason with others I think it my duty to write and speak the more about it where I come, that Friends and others may be better informed. Some have insinuated, as if the Primitive Saints kept Captive Slaves; this is hellish Censure indeed, to accuse the greatest of Saints with the greatest of Sins; whose Damnation is just, and their reward shall be according to their Works; for they were without Spot, then free from the greatest Spot; holy, as God is holy; perfect, as he is perfect; God Sanctifieth, and they that are Sanctified, are one. Blessing Honour, Salvation and Glory to our God, forevermore, Amen, saith my Soul.

And now my dear Friends and others, you that came in Servants to this Country, and Slaves, although for a short time by your own Consent too, for you to plead for Slave Keeping, is almost intolerable.

I say, you that came here poor, vile, miserable wretches, destitute and forlorn, and here you were kept to hard Labour, which was good for you, and brought you to a sense of your filthy, abominable, undone, and woeful cursed condition which you, many of ye had been in, then O then many of you came to consider of your ways, and were wise in turning to the Lord, into your own Hearts by the moving and rising of his own blessed Light, Life, Grace and pure Love there in your own Souls, which was as a Light shining in a Dark Place, your Hearts dark indeed, by reason of Sin, and that filthy Life which you had lived; you came to be burdened with it, and seek relief in turning to the Lord in your Hearts, where he was and is to be found, blessed be his pure Name which is his Essence or divine Nature, manifest within Men; so when you came to this good experience, you came to love the Society of Friends and follow the good example of our worthy Elders, very commendable in you to do, which first settled in this Country; you came to live sober lives, and by your industry, the Almighty favouring, some attained to very large possessions here, being a large Country and few People, but now more numerous, so no occasion for Slaves; for had this Land been covered with 'em as it is now in some Places, and too much here already, how would you have come to this greatness; you might have perished for want of Business to purchase necessaries. Let it never be forgotten by you, I beseech and pray ye for the Lord's sake, and for your own and your Children's sake, that are coming up in vast Numbers, as well as them that are, or may become Servants hereafter, with many, yea very many of your own Children, which is very likely by the wicked soul courses many of our Youth take, they may be brought to the same Misery and extremity as you were, by their foolish Lusts and Vanities; my Soul mourns in contemplating of it, and is in sore distress and misery, with many of my dear and inwardly beloved Friends, Male and Female, on this sad Account, as well as other gross Sins, many dear tender Souls in our Society, reproachfully called Quakers, have writ and bore Testimony against this Sin at times, near 50 Years, but were reproached for that likewise; but some are gone to their Graves in Peace; many yet living; as in Pennsylvania, Jersey, Long Island, Nantucket, Old England, which I have been with at their Houses, and their Writings are extant at this time to my certain knowledge, although many poor seeking Souls, that are bewildered by this wicked Hellish Sin in our Ministers, Slave Keeping, will not believe or cannot believe it, but rather believe we approve of it as a People with one consent unanimously. When some Friends have been reasoning with some Sober People of other professions in my hearing, concerning the Pride and Covetousness of their hireling Preachers, and concerning Truth's Principles, they have had nothing to say for the one, or against the other; but whether shall we go, say they, we do not approve or like keeping Slaves, it is not doing as we would be done by ourselves; and your People are as greedy as anybody in keeping Slaves for their Gain, (it is too true) But not all said I, now say they again, who shall we believe, we are sure and do know, that your Preachers and Elders, Chief Leaders have 'em; answer was made not all, for some have testified against it, as a very heinous Sin, for many Years, Year after Year; and are gone to their silent Graves in Peace, and many yet living amongst us, as above is mentioned. Why then, say they, do you not separate. Here it is thus written, "Wherefore come out from amongst them, and be ye separate, saith the Lord, and touch not the unclean thing; and I will receive you. (2 Corinthians 6. 13-17) Read the next verse with attention, in the fear of the Lord.

I know no worse or greater stumbling blocks Evil has to lay in the way of honest Inquirers, than our Ministers and Elders keeping Slaves; and by straining and perverting Holy Scriptures, Preach more to Hell, than ever they will bring to Heaven, by their feigned Humility and Hypocrisy.

Falsehood works wonders, by a seeming Gospel Ministry of great repute; for by keeping of Slaves, the Slave Keepers carry on an evil Work. A false and fallen Ministry has been the greatest Instrument of Evil. As may be seen in George Fox's Journal, and in many more beside, which I have by me. I have understood lately, that some have made their Wills when they were Sick, to set their Slaves free at such an Age, 30 or 40, after their Death; that will not salve the Sore, it is too deep and rotten, God will not be mocked so, nor Wise Men neither. It is written, when the time of Pentecost was fully come, there were People of many Nations gathered together, to hear the Apostles, and all heard in their own Tongue the wonderful Works of God. And if they were now here in Pennsylvania, they might hear and see the works of

Evil; Men and Women preaching up the Purest Religion in the World, and live in the greatest of Sins at the same time, the Mother of Enormities, *says Benjamin Lay.*

I do firmly believe in the Secret of my Soul, before the Lord, that Slave Keeping and Trading, with what has and now does daily attend and appertain unto it, is a cause of Great Sins as anything ever was in the whole World.

The 30th of the 10th Mo. 1736. I did not know but I had done Scribbling about Slave Keeping, but this Day I called to see our Friend J.R. at his House in Philadelphia, who was newly arrived from Bristol, in Old England; and he speaking of the Slave, or Guinea Trade, said, while he was in Bristol (Bristol was an important Quaker center) four or five Weeks, there was fitted out for that Trade nine Sail; and he told me according to Account he had there, that there goes from Bristol about 50 Sail in a Year for Slaves: and I suppose some plain Coat Men (Quakers) are concerned in it there as well as at Liverpool, Barbados, and elsewhere; now if each of these 50 Vessels carries 300, some carry many more, it comes to 15,000 Souls Yearly, Stolen by Bristol Men; and if there should be four times as many Stolen by Vessels from London, Liverpool, North Britain, Ireland, Barbados, Jamaica and some other Places, as I suppose there may, it comes to 75,000 Yearly, Stolen and kept in Iron Furnaces; so that in 50 Years and more since Friends have been concerned in this practice, beside what has been increased by Generation, comes to 3,825,000.

Is not this ten times worse than the Sins of the Commerce of Slaves in other places and times?

So I inquired of the Friend what they did with this or such vast Numbers of Slaves; he said, they carried them to Jamaica generally, and sold them to the Spaniard for the Mines, or anybody else, I suppose, that will give most for them, although they keep them and their Posterity, in their cursed Hellish Iron Furnace for evermore.

O False Christians for Evil, and Protestants too! This is only the way to show others of their notorious Wickedness and inhumanity, when we encourage them in it all we can, by supplying of them with Slaves, for our cursed Gain.

Several Eminent Friends amongst us of great Note, have boasted in my hearing of having Servants or Slaves born in their House. May not Truth say that our Preachers and Elders,, Keepers and Traders in Slaves do this for nothing but their ungodly Gain. But what will our Wicked Slave Keepers get by flying beyond the Gospel and the Law, to justify their cursed infernal practice.

Now Friends, you that are Slave Keepers, I pray and beseech you, examine your own Hearts, and see and feel too, if you have not the same answer from Truth now within; while you Preach and exhort others to Equity, and to do Justice and love Mercy, and to walk humbly before the Lord and his People, and you yourselves live and act quite contrary, behave proudly, do unjustly and unmercifully, and live in and encourage the grossest Iniquity in the whole World.

For I say, you are got beyond the Gospel Law to do Evil. You have many Thousands of Slaves, or caused 'em to be so, and for ought I know many Hundreds of Thousands, within 50 years.

What do you think of these Things, you Gospel Ministers that keep poor Slaves to Work for you to maintain you and yours in Pride, Pride and much Idleness or Laziness, and Fullness of Bread? How do these Things become your plain Dress, Demure Appearance, Feigned Humility, all but Hypocrisy, which according to Truth's Testimony, must have the worst place in Hell; to keep those miserable Creatures at hard Labour continually, unto their old Age, in Bondage and sore Captivity, working out their Blood and Sweat, and Bowels, youthful strength and vigour, then you drop into your Graves, go to your Places ordained or appointed for you; so leave these poor unhappy Creatures in their worn out old Age, to your Proud, Dainty, Lazy, Scornful, Tyrannical, and often beggarly Children, for them to Domineer and Tyrannize over, cursing them and you in your Graves, for working out their youthful Blood and strength for you, and then leave 'em to be a Plague to us; and then of the abuses, miseries and Cruelties these miserable old worn out Slaves go through, no Tongue can express starved with Hunger, perish with Cold, for want of everything that is necessary for an Humane Creature. Dogs and Cats are much better taken care for, and yet some have had the Confidence, or rather Impudence, to say their Slaves live as well as themselves.

Such notorious Lies will never ho down well, with any Sober right, tender hearted People truly fearing God, and that love the Truth above all; for such I believe firmly, when they come to see, and rightly consider the vileness of this practice in all its parts, and the cursed Fruit it brings forth, they will never enter into it; and if they are in, will endeavor to get out as soon as they can; for I do believe if all the Wickedness Tyranny, Oppressions and Abominable Barbarities were written concerning this Hellish Trade, it would fill a large Volume.

Many have said, they do not see that Slave Keeping is not so great an Evil or Sin, who are so Blind as them that will not see; but I think it is my duty to inform those that are willing to see by Word and Writing, and then leave it to the Lord.

There has been that which has reflected on me, as if I wanted a Party, to see what Numbers I could get on my side; the living God Almighty is Witness for me. I desire no Party, no Number but what is on the Lord's side but which holds the Blessed Truth in righteousness and holiness of Life, and in the Truth. I must confess I choose that Number, though but 5, then 500 that hold the Truth in unrighteousness; and though I could get the Friendship of the World and worldly Spirits, even them amongst ourselves and all their wealth beside; which have the iniquity of Slave Keeping. My witness is in Heaven; but I must expect a great many more Slanders than these.

But my dear Friends, as to my own part, if the Lord has stirred you up against me, let him accept of an offering; but if it be only Men, I don't fear in the least;

but my dearest God, whom I serve with pure Love, fervently, will deliver me, and in his own Blessed time establish me in my Inheritance with Saints in the Light. O that the Lord my God would be pleased to raise up some Worthies that be Valiant for the Truth, upon Earth, and bring them forth into open view, in Sight of all Men, for his Name sake, which is the Truth.

O that we may never sell our Birthright, for a morsel of Meat or any Advantage of this beggarly World. Doth Truth lead its Ministers to keep their fellow Creatures in Bondage and sore Captivity, and their Offspring forevermore. If it does not, but the practice be proved by the Blessed Truth itself to be contrary and directly opposite to its divine Nature, as to be sure it is. Why I pray and beseech you my dear Friends, are some that seem to be Truth's Ministers, so Angry, in a Rage, and such as Fury, as many have been, and are to my knowledge, when they have been reproved for, or opposed in this their wicked Sin, and very great Iniquity; for so it is proved by Truth itself.. Who dare judge a Minister, he will be in such a Fury if he is not true, although he pretend to be a Servant in the Church to us all. I know what I write by large experience, for many Years, in several Nations, where my lot hath been cast; so that I am not as one that beats the Air in this cause as concerning false Ministers; but as to Truth's Minister, that always dwells in Truth and follows Truth wheresoever he goes, Truth bears witness in me, that I love them and the pure dear sweet Testimony Truth has given us, better than all things in this vain World. O that these Things were well considered by all Preachers and hearers; and that no Preacher might be suffered to appear in our Meetings, but such as were clear of this Sinful Practice, Slave Keeping; then we should have but few Preachers for a time, I think, but much better Preaching. Dear Friends, I myself do consider how it stands, and what I may have to encounter with; but shall leave all to my dear sweet and forever blessed Rock. Is it not the Church's right, to judge of the Ministry and Ministers, and to call them to strict Account, concerning their Doctrine, Principles, Practices and manner of living? *Says Benjamin Lay*

Abington, the 5th of the 7th Month 1736. It was well said of one. A glorious and precious thing indeed, is true Unity; but I know no stronger Bulwark Evil has against it, in the Church of Christ, than Slave Keeping, and all the train of abominable Filthiness, which does and will attend it, and is inseparable from it (especially in Ministers) who by their foul Example have lead (I suppose) many Hundreds, if not Thousands into the Snare, and will many, yea very many more, if there is not some more effectual and speedy care taken to prevent, withstand and suppress so potent an Enemy as it is, both in Church and State. What I pray and beseech you, my dear Friends, whose Love and Unity in the Gospel Fellowship, which is sweet and precious, easy to be entreated, this I say is what I desire more than all the World, or a Thousand Lives, let People say what they please of me or my Proceedings, for the Truth's sake, and all my fellow Creatures present and eternal Welfare, my witness is in Heaven, and in many of my Truth's dear Friends whose Unity is precious to me and sometimes overcoming, in the pure precious Life of the Lamb; what, I say, will become of the innumerable Offspring that is coming up, if all should have Slaves to do their Work within Doors and without, as many have, they might or may perish for want of Business, to get a Piece of Bread or a Coat to put on, in the next Generation, and so on without end. O hard Lot! I have been often asked what shall we do? If it is so hard now, what will you do when they are more increased, for they grow on us, as in other Places.

Well, my dear Friends, I can truly say with great Sincerity, I write these things, not to offend, but to inform, caution, and advise them that are concerned, to pray to the Lord for Wisdom and Strength of Faith, to quit their Hands of them before it is too late; a Day of Vengeance will come.

We are apt to blame Pirates for Stealing some of our Goods and Merchandise, and it may be they have been brought up and instructed in that, that is a hundred times worse, that cursed Guinea Trade.

O! O! That my Soul could find some relief, for the distress that it hath been in, for 17Years and more at times, on this sad Account; but if Friends will not hear, O believe me, mine Eyes shall weep sore in Secret. *Benjamin Lay*

Because the Lord's Camp is in Captivity, for they that keep Captives, are in Captivity and Bondage, and brings many of their Friends, Male and Female into Bondage, because of Sin, and continuing in it.

Your Fathers have built a Wall of Iniquity, and you are daubing it with untampered Mortar, in Keeping

Slaves and pleading for it; O vile and shameless practice, which we ought to be separated from, especially Ministers and Elders, whose example is ten times worse than others; such worthy Friends as them! So here the Leprosy spreads, and it spreads more and more. Dear Friends what shall we do in the end thereof? For my dear Friends , I think it is easy to prove that there is as great disproportion between Slave Keeping, take it root and branch, and all the sad Fruit it brings forth, as there is between Light and Darkness, Christ and Hell.

How can we expect the Holy preference of our God to go with us, if we keep our Fellow Creatures in everlasting Bondage, them and their Wives and Children. Many eminent Persons have been carried away with Slave Keeping—Preacher's bad example and sound Doctrine, and many more will I fear be so; O the Ministry, the Ministry is corrupted. Then we shall know that War and Fighting, Killing and Stealing and receiving Slaves, and Souls of Men, cometh of our Lusts, which warreth in our Members, against the pure Holy Spirit of God in our Hearts.

O my beloved Friends, can a Minister of the Gospel, of Jesus Christ, which is the Power of God, keep Slaves and not be an Enemy to the Holy Cross of Christ; my Friends, I can freely call you, that are born again, and truly fear God, and love God's pure Truth more than all, of what Nation or Profession so ever you are, you I do believe abhor this vile practice, much more to be found in it. Dear Friends, I have been for many Years, almost 20 before I ever saw Pennsylvania, closely exercised, and sorely oppressed with a false and forward Ministry, where Slave Keeping is not permitted by Law, and has been, I firmly believe, a great means of bringing in and spreading the Apostasy, and so continues to do, by some that pretend to preach freely, as well or ill as by the bare faced Hirelings of our time, who cannot deny but that they make a trade of Preaching for their Bellies, but gross Apostasy by the way.

I have had it in my mind for a considerable time, to write something concerning a false Anti-Christian Ministry and a true Christian Ministry, fitted and sent forth by the Spirit of Truth itself, in this our Day, with the Epistles of many worthy Men, of several persuasions, on that Subject; but fearing it will swell this Volume too large, it is thought best to be reserved for another Impression, with something concerning the Kingdom of Heaven, what it is, and where it is to be found, with the most ready, sure and certain way to attain it, plainly describe; for the sake of the sincere in Heart, who are travelling toward Zion, with their Faces thitherward, of all persuasions, whose present and eternal welfare, I wish and desire for, as for my own Soul, of all Colours and Countries. *Benjamin Lay*

As no Man or Men can set forth in Words spoken or written, the great good, service, comfort, joy, strength and consolation, a true Ministry sent from God has been, and is of, for the building up of the true Church in God, in their most Holy Faith.

So no Men or Angels, nor all the Men in the World can declare to the full the great evil, that a false Ministry, has been, and is of, for the Building up of the false Church in their sinful and unholy Faith and Practice.

I had it also much in my mind to write something concerning the Lives of the Primitive Christians, mentioned by William Penn in his *No Cross, No Crown* which might be of Service, to them that live single Lives especially.

O the strict Rules of Temperance that was amongst those Quakers in Old England! What Persecution then was by Plundering, Robbing, and ruining of Families? What Whipping and Imprisoning, many Hundreds at a time, some suffocated to Death, some imprisoned during Life, some Banished, and in other ways Tortured.

Then about the same in New England, how many of our first dear and true Friends, called Quakers, suffered there by plundering and ruining of Families, Whipping and Banishing almost continually, with cutting of Ears, and Hanging there was in that Day, for the sake of the Testimony of or for the pure Holy unchangeable Truth, and of good Conscience, against all Iniquity, Cruelty, Bloodshed and Inhumanity, which was acted there, by them that had fled from Old England to save their Backs and their Purses.

Much more might be written concerning these and such things, which might fill many large Volumes. But this is not like Slave-Keeping; for those where dispatched or set at Liberty, and some cause pretended; but Slaves for no fault, so much as pretended, but only Evil Covetousness in the Stealers and Receivers, and then by a lingering Martyrdom from one twenty Years to another, some above Ground and some under Ground in Caves and Dens or Mines, are Murdered by Working hard, and Starving, Whipping, Racking, Hanging, Burning, Scalding, Roasting, and other Hellish Torments, very sorrowful to consider.

O when will there be an end of these Things, seeing it now going on with main strength by almost all parties, as well as by some of those that pretend to the most strict self-denying Doctrine in the World, that is so full of Mercy, Compassion, Forgiveness to the very worst of Enemies, Tenderness, Meekness, Mildness, Sweetness of Love, and Pity to all Creatures of all kinds; the merciful Man is merciful to his Beast. Yet some of these Pretenders to this Purity can join with these Men Killers and Stealers for Gain, which is hard to write, but this is True.

But I do know there is a faithful Remnant amongst the People called Quakers, in America, that are zealous against this and all other Iniquity, to whom my Soul is nearly united in Spirit, blessed be the Lord my God, for so great a favour for evermore, and I believe some of other Professions also, whom I dearly love; and I have some Hope and Number of all Sorts, that truly fear God and Love his Truth at Heart, will increase, which I should rejoice to hear and see, although Things seem to look dark at present. *Benjamin Lay*

Abington, the 3d of the 3d Month, 1736, between 3 and 4 this Morning. It was again revived in my Mind, the Practice of Slave Keeping, and thus to query. Whether it is not as wicked and sinful a Practice to keep and trade in Slaves, as to commit the Evils and filthy Abominations, which are not in Custom.

The 15th of the 1st month, 1736, 1737. I presented a Treatise concerning Hirelings in the Church to King George the 1st as I think there is as much need now to keep such as are of the same Spirit out of the Church, or it is in great Danger in the Opinion of some seeing Worthy Friends, who can see beyond Profession, Formality or worldly Interest.

That Spirit has something in view; the good of the Belly, a rich Wife or Husband, carrying on a good Trade, or to be exalted, and to get or keep up a strong Party for some Design, base enough; and under this Cloak of Deceit, accuse other of seeking opposition. Now when this Spirit goes forth with Authority from the outward Church, then our Meetings are or may be sure to be grievously pestered, with noise if not nonsense. It seems as if some of our Ministers have forgotten the great Benefit of Silent Meetings, if ever they rightly knew it, that they are so restless in them, and musty be hammering and hammering. The Nose of the Workman's Tool was not to be heard in Building the outward Temple, and much less the inward, which is the Work of God.

But if the Words be never so sound and orthodox, without Life they are but as Chaff; and what is the Chaff to the Wheat? Why truly, Friends, you know the Chaff is for the Beasts; but the blessed Wheat, with which our heavenly Father feeds his Babes, is for the Children of the Kingdom, New Jerusalem, the Church of the living God, God's House.

Many worthy Friends have been burdened with this scattering Spirit for many Years, especially its profaning if not blaspheming the sacred Name in Prayer. When our Meetings on First Days or others, are a little settled in Silence, and the Children in the Kingdom in their heavenly Places, and their Father begins to feed them, up stands a cracked Trumpet, with an uncertain Sound; or peradventure an old broken Cistern, with a little thick muddy Water at bottom, kept in for the Meeting, and there thrown out among the Children when in Truth it is hardly fit to hear. Now if such filthy Stuff be countenanced, encouraged and commended by our Elders and Ministers, some of them, what a Condition the is Church in, which should be without a Spot? I leave it to the Wife in Heart to judge, to such Ministers and Elders as rule well and are worthy of double Honour. So says **Benjamin Lay**

Abington, between 11 and 12, after a good Meeting at Oxford, where was 6 males and 4 contra. *Dear Friends:* I remember about 40 years ago I kept my elder Brother's Sheep, and the pretty Lambs and their Dams would be quietly sweetly and prettily feeding together, a very beautiful and comely Sight to see. But if a Stranger, my Friends, the Stranger, came near with his Dog, (the Dog sucks the Blood which is the Life of the Sheep) and if this Dog fell a barking yawling or howling, among the Sheep and the pretty pretty dear Lambs, immediately they leave their Feeding, and run for their dear Lives; so they would, be scatter'd, altho' there was or might be a great Flock of them together. Sometimes, I must confess, I have been a little careless and sleepy like some other Shepherds, and then the Sheep would go wandering about over Hedge and Ditch, and get into my Neighbour's Corn, and do Mischief; and then it was very hard for me to get them out of the Corn and into order again. Sometimes it would cost me many Tears before I could get them into order again. Sometimes if the Sheep and Lambs were not gathered together before Night, in the Night in the Dark the Dog would come and bite many of them, and suck their Blood, and some he would kill; so then that would be a Grief to the Owner, and a Reproach to the Shepherd.

So, my very dear Friends, you that are the right true Shepherds, that love the Sheep more than all things in this World, you can very easily make an Application, for it is your Life and Delight to take Care of your Father's Sheep, and his Lambs especially, and are grieved when the Dog, the Dog, the Bloodsucker, does but bark, and hinder them from Feeding. I know what I write, blessed be the Name of the good and great Shepherd, for evermore, who laid down his Life for his Sheep and Lambs.

My dear faithful Friends, you are much esteemed by me, and your Unity in the *Creator*, which is the Church, is much more desired by me than all things in this World, I can truly say. It has been much in my Mind for a considerable time, to lay before you my Concern for having some of our ancient worthy Friends Epistles of Warning, Reproof, Cau8tion, and Advice to Ministers, collected and reprinted; apprehending it may be of some Service to the Collection of such as I have mentioned, or such as you shall think will be of most Service; I earnestly desire and entreat to have your Advice and Counsel; for I know right well that in the multitude of Counsel there is Safety, especially with them dear Friends that know the Truth and are faithful; these are the best Counsellors in the whole World. I am your Brother and Friend in the blessed Truth. ***Benjamin Lay, Abington***

Abington, the 18th of the 2d month, about 6 or 7 at night. *Dear Friends,* As I was at work in the Garden, it came into my Mind, that many of our Preachers would or did make Preaching so common, that many of our young People, and old ones too, did not much matter it; nay I believe many, year very many, loath it; it is fulsome and burthensome to them, instead of edifying strengthening; by reason of many, I fear very many, going and running in their own Will and Time; which brings a very great Exercise, and many heavy Burdens upon some tender dear young Ministers, and others, which are rightly concerned, which cannot receive their chaffy Doctrine, but are almost choked with it, as well they may, for it is very killing to sit under their dead dry noisy dark dreaming in-and-out Harangues which brings Death and Darkness over our Meetings, such as may be felt. The Tongue of the Dogs was heard which darkens Counsel with or by Words without Knowledge being alienated from the Life of God, indeed through the Ignorance that is in them, because of the Blindness of their Heart. False Ministers are working in their Hour and Power of Darkness; if the Light that is in them be turn'd to Darkness, it is very great. Such are Wells without

Water Clouds without Rain, wandering dark Stars. One that hateth a Brother in Darkness, Darkness has blinded the Eyes. Some for a Damnation. The People are as Waters, very unstable, and so are ready to receive unstable and unsound Doctrine, although it may prove to their Destruction in time e'er they are aware, and utter Ruin of the Church, and People or Congregation. Oh that it might be prevented before it is too late, saith my poor soul. **B.L.** *Abington*

Abington, the 30th of the 2d Month, 1737. This Day as I was sitting at my Door, musing about or concerning the Miseries or Poverty of Humankind, it came into my Mind, that it is Ignorance and Idleness, Luxury and Pride, (not Temperance, Frugality and Industry; *with Parsimony,* as one said, *a little is sufficient, without it nothing*) which leads to Covetousness, and Covetousness leads to them; the one is the Cause, and the other the Effect. Riches, then Pride. Luxury and Pride, then Oppression and Covetousness to maintain it.

The 1st of the 9th Month, 1737. Early this Morning it was given me to see, that all Slave-keepers and Traders with them for Gain, were Apostates which pretended to be Christians; especially in Ministers it is a double Crime, because of their bad Example to their Flock; for all such have the Mark of the Beast, Prostitute and False Prophet on them, Let them preach as long as they will or may.

Oh faithful Friends! Thy Leaders cause thee to err, by their Lies and their Lightness! Oh how mine Eyes have seen some of the first Rank, sit and stand and laugh, Preachers and others, when I have been speaking of the Bondage and miserable Captivity of their poor Slaves, in as light and airy a many as any Boy in the town need to do: Persons Male and Female, eminent in the Church, Friends of Renown in their Generation and Congregation; long Custom and Covetousness having made the Sin, altho' so very gross, so easy and familiar to them. Some of which I do verily believe have known the pure Presence of the Divine God of Life and Glory, the holy Light and blessed Truth in their Souls; yet afterwards become vain in their Imaginations, to think Slave-keeping was lawful; so their foolish Hearts became darkened and hardened again worse than ever. Oh that is a sorrowful Condition, to have the greatest Mark of the Apostasy in the World, upon them, and not to know or believe it!

When I say *All Slave-keepers Apostates,* mean them that keep innocent Men, Women and Children in everlasting Bondage. As to petty criminals, that will not or cannot make Restitution, I think, as well as many other tender Friends and People fearing God and loving his Creation, their Fellow-Creatures, although very wicked, that they had better be kept in Bondage that by hard Labour they might be brought to Repentance and Amendment of Life, in order to a happy Death, than to put them to Death in their Sins; for in the Grave there is no Repentance; but hard Labour and mean Living is an Antidote to Luxury and Idleness, and Captivity and Reverse of Nature might prevent a great deal of Wickedness in the World, and bring many unthinking Creatures to remember and prepare for their latter End before it be too late, which I should rejoice to see. There is an excellent

Passage by *Ralph Sandiford*, from *Thomas Moore* High Chancellor of England, much to the purpose. Likewise that holy Man of God *George Fox* that faithful Servant, and indefatigable Labourer in the most high Lord's Vineyard, who turn'd more Souls from Darkness to Light than any one that *England* or the Dominions thereof, has produced since the Apostles Days, I do firmly believe, as his excellent Journal does make appear to them that can read it with the same divine Mind in which it was written, besides the multitude of faithful Testimonies to the Divine Power that wrought all his Works in him, and for him. While this dear Lamb George Fox as in Darby Prison in Persecution, he was under great Suffering of Spirit, and under the very Sense of Death, as he write, and he writ to the Judges about putting People to Death for stealing Cattle or Money, and small Matters, and thus it was:

> *I am moved to write unto you, to take heed of putting men to death for stealing Cattle or Money, &c. for the Thieves in old time were to make Restitution, and if they had not wherewith, they were to be sold for their Theft. Mind the Laws of God in the Scriptures and Spirit and gave them forth, and let them be your Rule in executing Judgment, and shew Mercy that you may receive Mercy from God the Judge of all. And take heed of Gifts and Rewards, and of Pride, for God doth forbid them, and they do blind the Eyes of the Wise. I do not write to give Liberty to Sin, God hath forbidden it; but that you should judge according to his Laws, and shew mercy, for he delighteth in the Judgment and in mercy. I beseech you mind these Things; and prize your Time now you have it, and serve him, for he is a consuming Fire.*

So far George Fox and much more concerning these things, when in Prison in persecuting Times. *Journal.*

Abington, the 2d of the 9th month, between 2 and 3 in the morning. The Thing appeared very clearly as at other Times, that Slave-keeping, with all its Concomitants, was the worst Idol, and one of the greatest Marks of the Apostasy, in the whole World, and the very worst Part of the great Prostitute's Merchandise, Mystery Babylon, the Mother of Prostitutes.

At this Time also it is brought to my Remembrance, with great Thankfulness to my dearest God, Redeemer and Preserver, the great Liberty that I with my Thousands more enjoy in this good land, which to many wise and right considerate People, is much more valuable than natural Life; especially our religious Liberty; with the Plenty of all good Things needful for the Body, which many hundreds of Thousands have been and are deprived of, by the above named vilest, grossest and blackest of all Abominations. And for this dark Scene to be acted by them that pretend to the most pure, holy, meek, sweet and loving Principle (to all People) in the World, is to some, yea many tender hearted People beyond compare with anything in the World; I say, for these People that pretend not to preach or to pray without the sweet holy Motion or Moving of the pure hold Spirit in their Hearts, the Unction from the Holy One, the sweet anointing Oil, the Feeling of which doth unite the Brethren.

Praises be given to God's pure Name, for the glorious and pure Presence in the holy Temple! For such bodies and souls are the Temple of the Holy Ghost, in the holy living God; but he or she that defiles this Temple by *Slave-Keeping,* they may God destroy, if not repented of and forsaken; can these sanctified and washed ones, that have been array'd with the fine Linen clean and white, clean and white indeed, which is the Righteousness of Saints; can these, with the Sow that is washed, turn again to wallow in the Mire of the Heathen Practice, *Slave-Keeping,* and worse, all things well considered; or like the Dog, a ravenous Beast, to lick up the filthiest and most unnatural Part or Sort of Excrement; and so is the Slavekeeping Practice, I am very certain.

Abington, the 8th of the 10th Month. This Morning very early it sprung again afresh and very lively in my Mind, concerning Marriages made in sweet Love, Fear, Wisdom and Counsel of the almighty living God if we want Riches and Honour, Pleasure and Joy. What is comparable to those Marriages made only in the Lord, in the Church, in Heaven, in the Temple; but few such Marriages I fear are to be found now a Days, that are made by the God in Heaven, which is the Truth.

Can there, my dear and well beloved Friends, be a better God or Holy Spirit than that that leads into all Truth, which is Heaven itself, and so into all Peace and Joy. I have had several other things of moment for a long time moving in mind, concerning the sweet comfortable and happy Life, Mankind might live, in Joy and if he would follow the inward true and spiritual Guide, which would never lead to wrong if strictly following its Counsel.

Christ was not ashamed to call such spiritual Souls is Brethren and Sisters, which worship God in Spirit, and in the Church. *I will declare thy Name unto my People; and after* his blessed Resurrection sent forth a Woman Preacher the very first, to declare of it, and I believe to preach freely as she had freely receiv'd of him; *So tell my people I am risen, and that I ascend to my God and your God.* O glorious Message! One of the best that ever was, and yet sent by a Woman! The glad Tidings of great Joy, that their Lord was alive that they thought was dead.

Although I have writ thus much for Women's Preaching, yet I would have none go before they are sent of the Lord, no more than Men. Male and Female are all one in Christ the Truth, the true Church or Congregation which is in God, and God in the Church which is his, where God rules and reigns, and is blessed for evermore. *So be it.* **B.L.**

Abington, the 22ⁿᵈ of the 12ᵗʰ mo. 1737,8. This Morning early, after five Days and Nights Fasting, I was considering the many Calumnies which the World or People of the World, has cast upon the Saints and Servants o the Living God, my very dear true and faithful Friends in Christ, called *Quakers,* as if they kept Slaves, or encouraged and connived at it for their Interest, Favour or Affection, or some base sinister Ends. But it is a mere Slander, for they abhor the Practice, and dare not touch with it, a verily believing it to be one of the grossest Sins and

Iniquities (with all Concomitants) in the whole World.

Objection. But some may have objected in my Hearing, that some, yea many called *Quakers,* and their Preachers, Elders and chief Leaders & Rulers, *Men of Renown in the Congregation.*

Answer. But I answer some were Apostates, Vagabonds and Impostors, and they were some of the worst Enemies, the very worst what is mentioned in holy Scripture plentifully by the holy Prophets.

And so it was amongst the Primitive Christians, about the Time of the Ten Persecutions, when they gat a little Ease from the Heathen Tyrants, the apostate Christians went to the same devilish Work, of murdering and butchering the true Christians, about their Creeds, keeping of Easter, the other Idols, and about the Clause of one Substance and two Substances, as if the eternal Being could be divided; But especially after *Constantine* the Roman Emperor was converted to the Christian Faith, in his Zeal he gave such large Donations and Revenues to the Church, that it is recorded, the same Day there was a voice heard from Heaven, crying aloud, *This Day is Poison poured into the Church!* Which the Event soon after verified. By an ancient observation, *Religion brought forth Wealth, and the Daughter devoured the Mother;* it is the very same now. So when the Bishops, Preachers and Rulers grew rich and high, they centered in Pride, Idleness, and Fullness of Bread; then they went together by the Ears with might and main, striving who should be greatest; then to inventing setting forth the old, nasty, fulsome, stinky Prostitute's Trumpery or Merchandise to Sale and they that would not buy it, oar could not receive it, might expect to be set out of the World by all the Tortures that Wrath and Hell could invent, as they could prevail with Kings, Rulers and Governors to afflict them, by unrighteous Laws and Edicts. And when the Magistrates were such Fools as to dance after their Call, they embroiled the whole Nations and Kingdoms in Blood.

Objection carried a little further concerning some that go under the Name of Quakers, keeping Slaves.

I answer with *Romans* ii. Courteous and gently Reader, please to read the whole Chapter in the Fear and Love of God, and in the Light of Truth, and thou wilt find and feel excellent Matter in it.

Philadelphia, the 25th of 12th mo. 1737, 8. This being the ninth Day of my Fasting, having taken nothing but a Draught of Spring water several times a Day, and am as well in Health as ever since I came to Pennsylvania, which is six Years this Spring, it lies on my mind to say something concerning Extortion, in paying or receiving Interest for Money, which I have been under Exercise about a considerable Time; and I could be heartily glad that our Friends as a Society would wholly set it aside, altho' I have something considerable upon Interest myself my Hands, and weakly in Body, and pretty well in Years, being near sixty.

Abington, 30th of the 2d month, 1738, This Morning, as I was preparing to go to Meeting, it was opened in me That all the nominal *Quakers,* who live in Sin, are of the same Spirit and as bad as other People in and of the World, and some of them much worse. Such as have been enlightened, and are sunk into the Earth again, are more dark and stupid than others; for Publicans and Prostitutes stand more ready and willing to receive the Message of the Kingdom of Heaven, which is Righteousness, Peace, and Joy in the Holy Spirit than they; and the Observation of the Children of God and keeps their Habitation in the Light. **B.L.**

Now I say my dear, inwardly and entirely beloved Friends, my Joy and my Crown, and my exceeding great Reward for all my Labours, and small Sufferings, is and I trust ever shall be your Unity, in the holy spotless eternal *TRUTH,* which I prefer before all my chiefest Joys in this World, my sweet God is Witness for me. **B.L.**

My dearly Beloved, search and see, weigh it in the Balance of the Sanctuary, in the Light of Truth, without which you know we cannot see clearly, nor judge impartially.

See, I say, is there by anything more black, more gross and dangerous or likely to destroy the Body and Branches and lay it entirely waste; although I know the root shall and will abide forever, and shall spring up elsewhere; it all the lame, dry, withered, sickly and dead Branches should be cut off by some judgment from above, and the whole Body dissected and Buried in Oblivion. Which I shall pray with my whole Soul and Spirit that it may be prevented for the sake of some that are living Branches, sweet, green and fruit-bearing amongst us. Inquire strictly dear Friends if there be any thing more likely to bring sudden Destruction upon us, than the Evil Practice of SLAVE-KEEPING.

And a False and forward Ministry, & that dark dry earthly Spirit that gives Life to it, and strength, and Worship ;the Images :& Idols, that it makes & almost the Image Makers; but they shall all have their part in the Lake, except they repent in time, which I heartily desire they may.

ABINGTON, the 18th of the 3d Mo. 1738. A Close Concern came in my mind early, very early this Morning, for the sake of Mankind, and the good Welfare and Preservation of Posterity, which a right and perfect way Instructing and Educating Youth, would tend much to the Furtherance of; and I know not any better way than that which would be the most likely and certain way to bring 'em to the knowledge of Divine Wisdom, the Work of the Spirit in their own Hearts, which Pride and Idleness very much obstructs, for as an excellent Author well observed, *Divine Wisdom begets Humility, but that which is acquired by the Learned begets Pride.* I say, the Humble God teacheth, but rejecteth the Proud.

So then Divine Wisdom exceeds all Literature and Human Wisdom, so far as Light excels Darkness, Heaven exceeds the Earth; for Divine Learning and Heavenly Wisdom, bring us to the Knowledge of our Maker, and to have sweet Communion with God, as the Saints had, who could say their Fellowship was with God. This, this Wisdom, my fellow Creatures of all Names, to this Learning, I do dearly, heartily and tenderly invite you, to this Fellowship, this Unity, Union and Communion.

I say, to have this most sweet, near, inward, intimate and perfect Fellowship, Acquaintance and Conversation Day and Night, at all times with God, and with God's dear Children born again, this is Heaven itself, the Kingdom of God is known to be within, not known without above the Skies; in his dear Children, new Moulded, new Made, new Fashioned.

I heartily wish we might be brought with one accord by Fasting and Prayer, in Spirit and in Truth, Night and Day, in Publick and Private, seek to and beseech the Almighty Lord of Heaven and Earth that God would be pleased to assist us with Strength and Courage to make War with, and engage against so Capital an Enemy that is so dishonourable to God, and all true Religion, destructive to Government and Mankind in general; for I do believe here is in this Land of America, as selfish, sordid, greedy, Covetous, Earthly minded People of almost all names, as any in the World.

The People in these Countries of America, have been Blessed with a great deal of Plenty and quiet living for many Years; it is to be feared many, yea the greatest Number by far are grown lukewarm, as to Religion especially, and are become careless, forgetful and negligent to make suitable returns to the Almighty for innumerable favours which hath been pleased to shower down upon us continually in such abundance, both Spiritually and Temporally for Body and Soul. I believe there was a time when many tender Souls (I hope there is some yet left) lived in a Divine Sense of these great Blessings, and sincerely endeavoured to make suitable returns or acknowledgments to the Lord, the Giver, for the same; by walking and living an Holy, Pious, Temperate, Righteous, Just and a Strict self-denying Life, and so manifested their Sincerity and Love to the ever Blessed *TRUTH,* in the sight of God and Man.

The young ones they are got into the airy Region: Riding, Drinking and Galloping about from House to House, Smoking, Snuffing, Chawing Tobacco, and other unclean fulsome, foul, indecent Practices; spending precious time in wasting the Substance and Estates, which they never wrought for, live and die miserable, and leave their poor Children Forlorn and helpless for others to maintain by their Intemperance, Idleness, Carelessness and Slothfulness or altogether, and when they have so consumed their Substance, ride up and down to borrow of others, but take little care to pay it again.

Oh! That the poor tender young Creatures, and old too, that are still remaining, might consider in time and turn to the Lord by unfeigned Repentance and Amendment of Life that so those Evils and Misery, which otherwise will come upon them, might be avoided, is the hearty desire of my mind, and what is the end or intent of my Writing. As I have said, it has been in my mind a pretty many Years, something concerning the true Reformation, Preservation and Welfare, or well being of Mankind, Especially the well educating & instructing of Youth, after the best manner or method for the Conservation, and Happiness of Posterity. **B.L.**

There is no proportion between Twenty Pieces of Silver, and LIBERTY. The Commodity itself is the Claimer. Most are afraid to meddle with Gold, though they might have it at easy rates; lest it should have been wrongfully taken from the Owners, it should kindle a fire to the Consumption of their whole Estate. 'This pity there should be more Caution used in buying a Horse, or a little lifeless dust; than there is in purchasing Men and Women: Whenas they are the Offspring of GOD and their Liberty is, ----*Auro pretiofioromni.* And seeing GOD hath said. *He that Stealeth a Man and Selleth him, or if he be found in his Hand, he shall surely be put to Death.* Exod. 21.16 This Law being of Everlasting; Equity, wherein Man-Stealing is ranked amongst the most atrocious of Capital Crimes; What louder Cry can there be made of that Celebrated Warning, *Caveat Emptor!*

And all things considered, it would conduce more to the Welfare of the Province, to have White Servants for a Term of Years, than to have Slaves for Life. Few can endure to hear of a African's being made free; and indeed they can seldom use their Freedom well; yet their continual aspiring after their forbidden Liberty renders them Unwilling Servants. It is likewise most lamentable to think, how in taking Africans out of *Africa,* and selling of them here, That which God has joined together, Men do boldly rend asunder; Men from their Country, Husbands from their Wives, Parents from their Children. How horrible is the Uncleanness, Mortality, if not Murder, that the Ships are guilty of that bring great Crowds of these miserable Men and Women. Methinks when we are bemoaning the barbarous Usage of our Friends and Kinsfolk in Africa, it might not be unseasonable to enquire whether we are not culpable in forcing the *Africans* to become Slaves amongt ourselves. And it may be a question whether all the Benefit received by *African* Slaves, will balance the Amount of Cash laid out upon them; and for the Redemption of our own enslaved Friends out of *Africa*. Besides all the Persons and Estates that have perished there.

Refuting arguments for African Slavery:

Africans are brought out of Pagan Country, into places where the Gospel is Preached. Answer: Evil must not be done, that good may come of it.

Africans have Wars one with another: Our Ships bring lawful captives that in those Wars. Answer: For aught is know they be between Town and Town; Provincial or National: Every War is upon one side Unjust. An Unlawful War can't make unlawful; Captives. And by receiving. We are in danger to promote, and partake in their Barbarous Cruelties. I am sure, if some Gentlemen should go down to the *Brewsters* to take the Air, and Fish: And a stronger Party from *Hull* should surprise them, and sell them for Slaves to a Ship outward bound: they would think themselves unjustly dealt with; both by Sellers and Buyers. And yet 'tis to be feared, we have no other kind of Title to our *Africans*. *Therefore all things whatsoever ye would that Men should do to you, do ye even so to them; for this is the Low and the Prophets.* Matt. 7. 12.

The ancients bought Servants and Slaves with Money. Answer: Since the partition Wall is broken down by God, inordinate Self-love should likewise be demolished. GOD expects that Christians should be of a more Ingenious and benign frame of Spirit. Christians should carry it to all the World. And for Men obstinately to persist in holding their Neighbours and Brethren under the Rigor of perpetual Bondage, seems to be no proper way of gaining Assurance that God has given them Spiritual Freedom. Our Blessed Saviour has altered the Measures of the ancient Love-Song, and set it to a most excellent New-Tune, which all ought to be ambitious of Learning' *Matt. 5. 43,44. John 13.34.* These *Africans,* seeing they are the Sons and Daughters of the First *Adam,* the Brethren and Sisters of the Last ADAM, and the offspring of God; They ought to be treated with Respect.

Why should any be so very earnestly bent about getting Money? Doth any History mention any one that was ever made good by Riches?

These things are Now, Now, Now, going on in the World in a Spiritual Sense, as certain as ever they were acted by the fore-mentioned, and by Persons too that makes great appearance of Sanctity in Religious Performances, but it's Self, whatever their demure appearance may be, and for Mammon what is the worst and most mischievous Evil in the World.

These rich grown, ever poor, over wealthy, ever needy, ever grasping, never satisfied, brim-full yet always empty, ever Labouring, yet always Idle, ever diligent, yet always negligent, ever waking, yet eternally asleep, ever living, panting and breathing after more, more, more, a little more, I say ever living yet eternally Dead, and there let 'em lie and stink still, if they will not be awakened. But I had much rather they should.

These great and high Masters of misrule, don't care to be controlled in their way altho' they are ever so much out of the way, which is very great Weakness as well as Wickedness, that Men and Women will have their own way tho' to their own and others Destruction, but the case is such, they having been so long in Power and Repute, had in Honour, Men of renown in the Congregation, chief Rulers in the House of the Lord, won't be contradicted, but if any should or dare do so, let his concern be ever so great or burthen weighty, he may expect to be put in the Stocks, in the high Court of Benjamin, with little Benjamin their Brother. Oh! How often have I heard and seen these things done metaphorically, I am loth to say where, but if any one ask me I can tell 'em, there is that that rules in the Church, to be seen and heard of Men, and to show their or its Elocution, display their Eloquence, as in their Preaching so in this, some for Mammon, some for some other ends base and vile enough.

And a few there is still left amongst us (I firmly believe blessed be the Lord, that have not any thing so much in view as in all sincerity, to promote and exalt the Honour and Interest of TRUTH, the Peace and Tranquility of the True Church, and the present and eternal Happiness, Welfare and well-being of Mankind, in all Nations, Colours and Countries in the World, that they might be brought to the Knowledge of the TRUTH, and be saved from Sin, yet from all Sin, for that is possible and so from Wrath to come; but some are, yea, very many are pushed on, Headlong and Headstrong, with a furious raging fiery and mad Zeal, yet blind (not from *Colchester* two Weeks Meeting, to *R.J.* to *Philadelphia* Monthly Meeting) to separate *Sarah* And *Benjamin*. I pray in my Heart at this time, they all that are living that had any hand in it, may have their Reward according to their Intention. I think to leave 'em there with him, him, him, himself, that is able to do all things, and so is able to produce good Effects, from very bad causes, and say, Oh *(Deus Meus Omnia)* preserve my Soul.

Oh! That all the Libertines, loose Livers, the Publicans and Prostitutes, the Smoking Drunkards, all unclean Persons, Thieves and Covetous, Covetous the Covetous Earthly minded Idolator, The Superstitious, Formal and Nominal Christians, Preachers and Hearers, the young and old, old, the old Hypocrites too, if possible, I say if possible might be converted, translated, drawn out of that deep, dirty Ditch Hypocrisy.

And all the blind Zealots, and Superstitious Bigots, of all Names, their Nature and Spirit is the same, when invested with a little imaginary Power. How they will rage and persecute furiously them that oppose 'em, reprove 'em and will not submit to their

Rules, Orders and Laws, though never so unjust and thus it happened to many of our dear Friends called *Quakers,* in *Old* as well as *New-England,* and elsewhere, when they went into their Synagogues, Mass-Houses, or Idol Temples to reprove 'em for their Hypocrisy and Wickedness, in pretending to Worship him that laid down his Life for his Enemies and at same time preparing Laws to take away the Lives of His Servants, that came in his Name, to do his Will, as he the Holy one required it at their Hands I would tenderly advise, and earnestly entreat all my dear Friends to be very careful not to taste nor touch that Dust and Dirt, Persecution, which is the Serpents Meat and *Cain's* Mark. It is to Christ's Brethren and Sisters, and all his true Friends and faithful Followers, to do the will of their the Creator in God's Holy Church, Body, comprised of Sanctified Members, purified Hearts and Souls, washed and cleansed; and such as those did of old, and now doth perfectly known a new Birth, a being Born again of God, and in God that is True and is the very TRUTH itself the very pure Verity of Verities, the Eternal Essence in God only, not in any Book or Books, a Thousand Ship-loads of the very best of Books will do us no good, not the best of Professions, Ordinances, and Humane Preachers (much less the worst) will do us no good, except Male and Female be Born again they cannot see the Kingdom or Government of TRUTH, which is one this was and is and ever will be declared of by the Eternal TRUTH, to all that had, have and shall have Eyes, Ears and Hearts truly prepared to receive it.

LETTERS SENT BY BENJAMIN LAY

Abington, the 1st of the 4th Month, 1738. To J.C. of Horsham

Dear and Well-beloved Friend, it came in my mind early this Morning, once more to write a few Lines to thee, concerning the close exercise of Mind, that is now on me, and have been many Years, long before I ever saw Pennsylvania; concerning that pernicious destructive Spirit, that destroyer of much good in our Meetings, I say, that pernicious Spirit, that appears in a false, as well as a forward Ministry in our Meetings, to their great disturbance and annoyance, especially of the faithful, both Ministers and others. Oh! This mighty Monster (false Ministry) with his many Heads, Horns and Crowns, this Monstrous, Beastly Spirit in Men and Women, rising up out of the Sea, or People, this beast that had a Wound by a Sword, but does live, but it is the Life of a Beast, altho' it was wounded by the Sword of the Spirit, by some Convictions for gross Sins, but the deadly Wound being falsely healed, the Beast doth live and is alive, and reigns in full strength in them, and have got the Dragons Power and Seat, and great Authority, and the whole World wonders after the Beast, the Worldly mind, and dark earthly Spirit amongst us; then again there is seen a little Beast with two Horns like a Lamb, raising up out of the Earth, and it exercises all the Power of the first Beast, that went or came before it, being of the same Essence, Nature and Substance, formed in the same Womb, Born of the Same Mother, Mystery of Babylon, the Mother of Prostitutes, base born

Children, full of all, all, all iniquity. The very depth of the Mystery of Iniquity, Dear Friends is this little Beast with his two Horns like a Lamb, very demure in the outward appearance, seemingly Zealous for right Discipline and good order in the Church, very loving to Friends of Repute, Ministers especially, good and bad, and get to their Houses and Tables, the richest sort of Friends, and those of the greatest Note to be sure, and most Account in the World, that they may spread their Name and their Fame wherever they come or go, that they may be more securely, covertly, cunningly and hiddenly carry on their Design in the Church, in making of Parties to strengthen their own Interest in the Church and their Families, by Trading and great Dealing, either in Land or Goods, Executorship, or by whatever way or means Wealth may be obtained, to set up themselves, and furnish their Posterity with rich Wives and Husbands, that they may be great in the Earth: And this to be contrived, carried on, acted and done with the face and appearance of Religion and Sanctity, and under pretense of Preaching the Gospel too, this is the very Secret of Secrets, of the Mystery of Iniquity and the depth of Evil, which many Thousands amongst us I believe doth not see. We discover the single Eye, the cleansed Eye of the mind, that is opened and cleansed by the very Light and Power of Truth itself, and kept open too, and clean in by the Eternal Light and Life of Truth or else the Dirt of Dust of the Earth, may and will get in again, and stop the Eye up again, and make it more dark and blind than ever, never, never more to be opened, and this is a sad dismal State indeed for any to fall into, deplorable, never, never, never to be recovered.

They that are not right lie down in sorrow, tho' they hide it from others for a time, they feel it themselves, but having once began to Preach for some base End, they are ashamed to, and afraid to leave off, altho' they are convicted and condemned in their own Consciences, clearly and heavily, to be sure, and so it follows, he that doubts is Damned.

Now, My Friend, if there was such, and so much care, quietness, stillness, silence and awfulness in Building that outward natural House, Built by Men but for a time.

How much more abundantly had we need to be in an awful, reverend, holy, pure, still and quiet frame of mind, when we meet together in order for the Building up of this inward and Spiritual House, New-Jerusalem, whose Builder and Maker is God himself, the Eternal Truth, and none else but he, and he himself alone, which was and is, is, is, to come, the Alpha and Omega, the Author as well as finisher of our most Holy Faith.

I am sorry there is so much Reason to say and proof to be made, that there is amongst us many Foolish (if not right down sinful and wicked) Builders, that pretend to be Teachers too, that considers little of these Weighty Concerns and knows less; these are them that are Crucifying the dear Lamb in his Spiritual appearance, when they are still crying Hosanna with their sinful Lips in our public Meetings, to the wounding and piercing through the sides all true and faithful Ministers, and right Worshippers amongst us. **Benjamin Lay**

The 4th of the 4th Month. **Dear John**, this Morning I was in my Garden pulling up some Weeds, it came in my mind what was objected against me lately by one that ministers among us N.A. and hath done near 20 Years; that I was for setting up some Ministers, and pulling down others, Now, Dear Friend, I must confess I do not approve of a false Minister, much less to set him up, neither would I pull down the True by no means, nor touch the truly anointed to do them any harm, for they are very near to my Life I can truly say without any reserve, and I hope ever will be while I have a Being. But if one should ask any Friend, even a false Minister himself, if we might at any Time receive, should or ought to encourage a false Minister, or approve, join and unite with him in Prayer or in his Testimony, he would answer in the Negative, no, no, if not for Conscience yet for fear of shame or blame, but then, says he, who shall be Judge, why truly I may say if we have no Judgment in our goings and doings, we are in a very poor dark Condition, as well as othaer Peiole, as false Ministers and Prodigals would have us, that we might receive such Husks as they havea to feed Swine withal, but the True Children in the True Kingdom cannot feed on such chaff, if they offer to receive it by conniving at or seemingly approving of or joining with such Swine-Herds, in Prayer or Testimony they will be in danger of being Choked, for they themselves have not true Peace, evil cannot give them; now if any one offer to prove or make manifest their pretentions to

Preaching is all Deceit and Cheat, and their seeming seed Corn, nothing but Chaff and Husk, their Peace flies away at once, like Chaff before a strong Wind; this I have often seen in England here and elsewhere. This Chaff, Dear Friend, will not do for Children, the Beast, the Beasts, Beasts can feed on it, for it is agreeable to their Natures as Bread is to Children, like loaves its like.

Those that go forth with Sparks of their own kindling, shall lie down in Sorrow. I think, Oh that these would wait for the still, still Voice, that would direct them aright, when and what to speak to the People, and when to be silent; and not go forth in the hurry and bluster of their own Spirits, in their own Time, but wait in the Lord's Time: Nor in the Fire, nor the Wind, nor the Earthquake, where the pure TRUTH is not known, nor his Voice heard.

I say again, I wish those that have been so long plowing with their ill-matched pair of Creatures, and sowing the Field with diverse Kinds of Seeds, would, or could be prevailed upon, to stand still a little and be quieted, and look back and round about the Field, and see what sort of Plowing they have made, and what Sort of Seed they have sown, and what Sort of Grain is grown up; whether there is not 30, 60, or an Hundred Fold more bad than good, and if so, sure there have been a great deal of bad seed sown in the Field, or it would not have been so (I firmly believe). I do not believe it is all owing to the Badness of the Ground, but for want of honest Labour performed, by Faithful and True Labourers, and then to have good, weighty, sound clean, pure substantial Seed sown, without Mixture, in it, by such Seed Men and Women, and such I love as my own Soul, much more that which dwells and grows in them or in us, the pure eternal Truth. Now my Friend, let all the impudent, false, forward, restless, uneasy, bold, self-conceited, turbulent, noisy, clamorous, covetous, selfwilled Preachers, Plowers and Sowers in our Meetings, look over the Field where they have labored, and compare it with any of their Neighbour's Fields, and see whether it be in any better Condition than theirs, if not much worse, all things well considered. The Advantages we have had and the great Favours that have been bestowed upon us, more than any People in the whole World, that I know of, since the Apostle's Days.

Friend J.C. is it not written, if thou takest a Bird's Nest thou shalt not destroy the Dam, and the young; but shall let the Dam go; but some of these forward Spirits destroy all, lavish out all, leave their Nest empty of all good, not considering there should be Store of good Seed left for Increase; and are like the foolish Idolaters, that lavish Silver out of the Bag to enrich and beautify their Idols and are left poor and needy themselves. How contrary it is to be proud idle, lustful Flesh and Blood, what a Burthen it is to it, the very Thoughts of it, and yet how easy, light, sweet, safe and pleasant it is, when once well attained, as the dear Lamb Jesus declared, My Burthen is Light and Yoke easy. **Benjamin Lay**

The 2d of the 4ᵗʰ Month. Dearly beloved J.C., this morning early I opened the Bible, and met with Jeremiah xxiii.9 and read it to the End, with some

Concern, to think what will become of us as a People; and of those bold confident Persons, Male and Female, that dare to speak in the Name of the Lord, when God doth not, nor never did speak to them, and run and go, when the holy One never sent them; but it is to be feared there is many, yea, many amongst us that encourages 'em, and they are Friends of Note too, if I may call 'em Friends. I think dear Friend, I may say as one said, Oh that my Head were as Water, and my eyes Fountains for tears! That I might, Oh, that I might weep enough for the slain and the blind! That the Enemy hath blinded; indeed, for any Writing or Speaking will avail little, no, no, no.   **Benjamin Lay**

CONCLUSION

Courteous and Friendly Reader,

There is some Passages in my Book, that are not so well placed as could have been wished; some Errors may have escaped the Press, the Printer being much encumbered with other Concerns: thou art lovingly entreated to excuse, amend, or censure it as thee please: But remember that it was written by one that was a poor common Sailor, and an illiterate Man.
Benjamin Lay

ADVICES REGARDING SLAVERY TAKEN
FROM EARLY QUAKER DISCIPLINES

Minority groups or individual Friends (as illustrated by Benjamin Lay) passionately spoke or wrote in opposition to slavery and the slave trade in the late sixteenth and early seventeenth century. They would suffer censure, alienation and sometimes disownment from the main body of the Society of Friends. Yet in such passionate speaking "truth to power", Friends would become pioneers in the anti-slavery movement right up to the time of the Civil War. This transformation was remarkable especially as the Society of Friends made up a significant portion of the general population during the early period of settlement in North America. The following statements regarding testimonies against slavery within the various yearly meetings were garnered from the 1999 publication *The Old Discipline* by Quaker Heritage Press (16 Huber Street, Glenside, Pennsylvania).

Philadelphia Yearly Meeting

It appears to have been the concern of this meeting revived from time to time, with increasing weight to testify their entire disunity with the practice of enslaving mankind (and particularly to guard all in membership with us against being concerned in the purchase of slaves from the coasts of Africa) yet as we have with sorrow to observe that in some parts of our country, his shameful practice is still continued and connived at, we think it proper to revive the advices heretofore issued, and again exhort our members, to be no way accessary to this enormous national evil, but to discourage it by all the justifiable means in their power; it being obvious that wherever it prevails it tends to corrupt the morals of the people, so as not only in render them obnoxious to the displeasure of the Almighty, but deaf to his warnings, and insensible and regardless of his impending judgments. (1755, 1806)

We earnestly desire it may become the concern of our members generally, to use the influence they have with those who hold slaves by inheritance or otherwise, that they may be treated with moderation and kindness, and instructed as objects of the common salvation in the principles of the Christian religion; as well as in such branches of school-learning as may fit them for freedom, and to become useful members of civil society. Also that Friends in their several neighbourhoods advise and assist such of the black people as are at liberty, in the education of their children, and common worldly concerns. (1778)

Understanding that some in membership with us, either through inadvertence, or from selfish motives, have hired slaves to assist them in their business; we desire such to consider that in so doing they promote the unrighteous traffic, and oppose our testimony against it. Friends are also cautioned against acting as executors of administrators to estates where slaves are bequeathed; and doing anything whereby their bondage may be prolonged. (1774)

We are united in judgment, that the state of the black people, who have been held as slaves by any of us or our predecessors, calls for a deep inquiry and close examination, how far we are clear of withholding from them, what under such an exercise may be opened to our view as their just right; and we earnestly and affectionately entreat those in particular who have released any of them, to attend to the further openings of duty. Even if no such obligations to this people existed among us, it is worthy of our serious consideration, whether any object of beneficence is more deserving of our regard, than that of training up their youth in such virtuous principles and habits as may render them useful and respectable members of the community.

It is the sense and judgment of this meeting, that if any of our members are concerned in importing, selling, or purchasing; or shall give away or transfer any slave, with or without any other consideration than to clear their estate of any future encumbrance, or in such manner that their bondage is continued beyond the time limited by law or custom for white persons; and also those who accept of such gift or assignment; they ought to be speedily treated within the spirit of true love and wisdom, and the iniquity of their conduct laid before them. And if, after Christian labour, they cannot be brought to such a sense of their injustice, as to do everything which the monthly meeting shall judge to be reasonable and necessary for the restoring such slave to his or her natural and just right to liberty, and condemn their deviation from the law of righteousness and equity, to the satisfaction of the said meeting, that such member or members be testified against as other transgressors are by the rules of our discipline for other immoral, unjust, or reproachful conduct. (1774)

It appearing that, notwithstanding the many afflictive dispensations with which divine wisdom has seen meet to visit this land, many of its inhabitants are so deaf to the language of the rod, as to continue in the nefarious traffic for slaves to the coasts of Africa: and that the importation of them is still connived at this meeting, considering such a conduct as a bold and impious defiance of the Ruler of nations, and pregnant with the most alarming consequences to our country, earnestly recommends to the meeting for sufferings to embrace every suitable opportunity for advancing our testimony in this respect, and for calling the attention of the public mind to this awfully interesting subject. (1786, 1787, 1806)

New England Yearly Meeting

It is the sense of this meeting, that the importation of slaves from their native country and relations is not commendable nor allowable practice, and that practice is censured by this meeting. (1727)

We fervently warn all in profession with us, that they be careful to avoid being any way concerned in reaping the unrighteous profits of that iniquitous practice of dealing in slaves whereby, in the original purchase, one man selleth another as he does the beast that perishes, without any better pretension to a property in him than that of superior force, in direct violation of the gospel rule, which teaches everyone to do as they would be done by, and to do good unto all; being the reverse of that covetous disposition, which furnishes encouragements to those poor ignorant people to perpetuate their savage wars, in order to supply the demands of this most unnatural traffic, whereby great numbers of mankind, free by nature, are subjected to inextricable bondage; and which hath often been observed to fill their possessors with haughtiness and tyranny, luxury and barbarity; corrupting the minds and debasing the morals of their children, to the unspeakable prejudice of religion and virtue, and the exclusion of that Holy Spirit of universal love, meekness and charity, which is the unchangeable nature and the glory of true Christianity: We therefore can do no less than with the greatest earnestness impress it upon friends everywhere that they endeavor to keep their hands clear of this unrighteous gain of oppression. (1760)

It is recommended to friends who have slaves in possession, to treat them with tenderness, impress God's fear in their minds, promote their attending places of religious worship, and give those that are young, at least, so much learning that they may be capable of reading.

It is our sense and judgment, that truth not only requires that the young, of capacity and ability, but likewise the aged and impotent, and also all in a state of infancy and non-age among friends, be discharged and set free from a state of slavery; that we do no more claim property in the human race, as we do in the brutes that perish. (1773)

Agreed that no friend import, or in any ways purchase, dispose of or hold mankind as slaves; but that all those who have been held in a state of slavery be discharged therefrom; that all those be used well who are under friends' care, and are not in circumstances, through non-age or incapacity, to minister to their own necessities; and that they give those that are young such education as becomes Christians, and encourage others in a religious an virtuous life. (1773, 1780)

Baltimore, Ohio, & Indiana Yearly Meetings

The past efforts of our Society to elevate and improve the conditions of our fellow men (Indian and African races), and the beneficial results thereof, encourage the Yearly Meeting to recommend to our members generally to consider attentively, from time to time, what further help it may be right for us to extend to the Indian and African races. It should not be forgotten that the soil which yields so bountifully to us was once the home of the Indians, and furnished their rude support, and we may yet be justly their debtors. In relation to the descendants of the African race, we earnestly desire that those under the care of our members may be treated with kindness, and instructed in the principles of the Christian religion, as well as in such branches of school learning as may fit them to become useful members of society. Whilst we rejoice that property in man is no longer recognized by the laws of our country, we tenderly solicit Friends, on all proper occasions, to bear our testimony against all human bondage and forms of oppression. (1806)

New York Yearly Meeting

Due care should be taken that all our members are clear of being concerned ... in illegal trade, or in dealing in prize goods, and Friends are pressingly advised not to violate our testimony against war in any respect: it is also affectionately desired, that when any Friends are brought into suffering on this account, they may manifest a disposition comporting with our Christian profession. It is also affectionately recommended, that we duly consider, whether by dealing in, or consuming the produce of the labor of slaves, we are not supporting and encouraging the system of slavery: and we tenderly solicit a scrupulous attention to the manifestations of duty in relation to this important subject. (1856)

As it has been, and continues to be, the concern of our society to testify its disunity with the practice of enslaving mankind, if any of our members should be concerned in buying or selling, or should give away or transfer any slave, in such manner as to cause his service to be extended beyond the time limited by law or custom for white persons; and those who accept of such gift or assignment, or hold any descendants of slaves transferred in the manner before mentioned, or hire any from those who hold them in bondage, or take them by indenture, or otherwise, unless their freedom be first secured, they ought to be speedily labored with, in a Christian spirit; and if they cannot be brought to such a sense of their injustice as to do whatever the monthly meeting should judge reasonable and necessary to restore those injured persons to their natural and just right of liberty, they should be disowned.

Friends are desired to avoid any act by which the right of slavery is acknowledged; but it is not hereby intended to bebar them from the exercise of benevolence toward those who are held in slavery.

Friends who have youth of African descent under their tuition, are exhorted to treat them in a Christian manner, it being their religious duty to give them useful and necessary learning, to fit them for business, and to instruct them in morality and the principles of religion.

The state of those who have been held as slaves by Friends, or by their predecessors, calls for serious inquiry and close examination, how far they are clear of withholding from them, or their children, that a assistance which may be found to be their just right; and the descendants of those friends who have held them in bondage, are affectionately intreated to attend to the openings of duty on this subject. Even if no such obligations to this people existed amongst us, it is worthy of serious consideration whether there is any object of beneficence more deserving attention, than that of training up the youth of the injured part of the human family in such virtuous principles and habits, as may render them useful and respectable members of the community. (1810)

North Carolina Yearly Meeting

As a religious society, we have found it to be our indispensable duty, to declare to the world our belief of slavery to the Christian religion. It therefore remains to be our continued concern to prohibit our members from holding in bondage our fellow men.

If any in membership with us, shall hire any in slavery their master or mistress, to assist them in their business, it is the judgment of the early meeting, that, in so doing, they promote the unrighteous traffic, and oppose our testimony against slavery; ;and if they cannot be prevailed on to desist, monthly meetings are at liberty to disown them.

A proper regard to this testimony, would lead our members to avoid acting as executors or administrators to estates in which slaves are bequeathed, or being accessory to any step whereby their bondage may be prolonged.

If any of our members are concerned in selling or purchasing, or shall give away or transfer, any slave, or accept of any such gift or assignment, so as to prolong his or her slavery, or prevent such from the benefit of their labour; they ought, speedily, to be treated with, in the spirit of love and wisdom, in order to convince them of the iniquity of their conduct; and if, after such Christian labour, they are not brought to such a sense of their injustice as to do whatever the monthly meeting shall judge to be necessary for the restoration of such slave to his or her natural liberty, and condemn their deviation from the laws of righteousness and equity, to the satisfaction of the said meeting, such shall be disowned. (1822)

Virginia Yearly Meeting

It is agreed that the meetings for sufferings shall consist of twelve members, chosen by the yearly meeting, and four by each of the quarterly meetings, and be subject to the following rule: To appear in defence of the rights of black people or their descendants, who have been liberated by friends; and such other people of colour as the yearly meeting may from time to time submit to its care. (1814)

As a religious society, we have found it to be our indispensable duty to declare to the world our belief of the repugnancy of slavery to the Christian religion; it therefore remains to be our continued concern to prohibit our members from holding in bondage any part of the human family.

A proper regard for our testimony in this respect also requires that we abstain from hiring slaves or purchasing them for a term of years, or undertaking to oversee them, as in so doing, the unrighteous commerce is promoted: and it is the sense of and judgment of this meeting, that where any of our members fall into such practices above mentioned, they should be labored with according to the rules of our discipline as in other cases of offence, and testified against by the monthly meetings if they cannot be prevailed upon to desist.

It is further advised that our members be cautious of acting as executors or administrators to estates where slabs are bequeathed; or of being accessary to any step whereby their slavery may be continued.

If any of our members shall be concerned in selling, or shall give away, or transfer a right to any person of colour or slave, or accept of any such gift or assignment, so as to continue their slavery they should be speedily labored with in order to convince them of the iniquity of their conduct; and if, after a due extension of Christian care, they cannot be brought to such sense of their injustice, as to do whatever cannot be brought to such a sense of their injustice, as to do whatever the monthly meeting shall judge necessary for the restoration of said slave to his or her natural liberty, and condemn their deviation from the law of righteousness, to the satisfaction of the meeting, such ought to be testified against as other transgressors.

It is advised, that those who have children of colour under their care, endeavor to instruct them in the principles of the Christian religion and give them a suitable literary education. (1814)

QUERIES REGARDING SLAVERY TAKEN FROM EARLY QUAKER DISCIPLINES

Are friends careful to maintain our testimony faithfully against slavery. (New England Yearly Meeting 1761)

Do they provide in a suitable manner, for those (former slaves) under their direction who have had their freedom secured and are they instructed in useful learning? (Baltimore, Ohio, and Indiana Yearly Meetings, 1821)

Are Friends clear of purchasing disposing of, or holding mankind as slaves, so as to prevent them from the benefit of their labor? Do they use those well who are set free and under their care, through non-age or otherwise, endeavouring to encourage them in a virtuous life? (North Carolina Yearly Meeting, 1822)

Do any friends hold slaves and do all bear faithful testimony against the practice, endeavouring to instruct the children of colour under the care in the principles of the Christian religion, and give them a suitable literary education? (Virginia Yearly Meeting, 1814)

QUERIES* REGARDING SLAVERY IN THE PRESENT TIME

Are we aware that slavery exists in the world today at a greater degree than in earlier times? (~) Do we recognize that slavery exists in many forms: chattel slavery, human trafficking, wage and debt slavery, conscription, sexual slavery, child slavery, addiction slavery, punitive incarceration and institutional execution? (~) Can we affirm the Truth taught by Paul that a person in bondage is "no mere slave but a true brother or sister both in the flesh and in Christ!"? (Philemon vs. 16) (~) Do we faithfully maintain Friends' testimony against slavery and work for the abolition of all forms of slavery in the present and future time?

*The reading of these Queries should be done in a thoughtful, contemplative manner. The (~) after each Query serves as a reminder of this concern.

Note: When our worship study group considered what might be included in *A Book of Discipline*. It was felt that we should acknowledge the fact that slavery exists in a greater degree in our time than ever before. We included a statement regarding this in the text with a footnote that:

"Friends were early pioneers in the efforts to abolish slavery. We are reminded that slavery still exists in the world today to a greater degree than in earlier times. Slavery comes in many forms: chattel slavery, human trafficking, wage and debt slavery, conscription, sexual slavery, child slavery, illiteracy, addiction slavery, etc. We are urged to renew our deep concern and work for the abolition of all forms of slavery in our time." The concern is that we not be comfortably complacent regarding this important testimony in the present and future as had been true in the past.

It was felt that by developing a module around the issue of slavery for *A School for Living: ...* (under the aegis of Joshua Evans' Trust) we might consider how we might understand and become involved as modern day abolitionists in working to end all forms of slavery. This module could be one way of honoring Benamin Lay through an institute honoring him in speaking to this concern. The module could be medium of educating ourselves about ancient and modern slavery, of action needed (including 'street theatre') and other means in speaking 'Truth to Power' regarding all forms of slavery in the human experience.

We adopted and updated the wording of that wonderful hymn written by 'The Quaker Poet", John Greenleaf Whittier, who was an ardent abolitionist of the nineteenth century. The Hymn can be sung to the tune of *O Perfect Love* or *Vesalius:*

Neighbor and friend, fold to thy heart another;
Where kindness dwells, the peace of God is there'
To worship rightly is to love each other,
Each smile a hymn, each kindly deed a prayer.

For them whom Jesus loved has truly spoken;
The holier worship which God seeks to bless
Restores the lost, and binds the spirit broken,
And feeds the widow and the fatherless.

Follow with reverent steps the great example,
Of him whose holy work was doing good;
So shall the wide earth be God's holy temple,
Each loving life a psalm of gratitude.

Then shall all shackles fall, the stormy clangor---
Of wild war carnage o'er the earth shall cease.
Love shall tread out the baleful fire of anger,
And in its ashes plant the tree of peace.

(The following material from the writings of Benjamin Lay has been condensed, the spelling updated – yet maintaining British colonial spellings of some words, and by changing some words into expressions more understandable to the modern reader.)

(One of the best historical studies regarding slavery is David Brion Davis' book *The Problem of Slavery in Western Culture* which won the Pulitzer Prize in 1967.)